Your First Grandchild

Your First Grandchild

The survival guide for every new grandparent

Claire Nielson,
Paul Greenwood
and Peggy Vance

Thorsons

An Imprint of HarperCollins*Publishers*

Thorsons
An Imprint of HarperCollins*Publishers*
77–85 Fulham Palace Road,
Hammersmith, London W6 8JB

The Thorsons website address is:
www.thorsons.com

Published by Thorsons 1999

Cartoons by Harry Venning

A catalogue record for this book
is available from the British Library

ISBN 978-0-7225-3698-8

Find out more about HarperCollins and the environment at
www.harpercollins.co.uk/green

I've made up a new name for you, Gran! I'm going to call you 'Old Bones'.

Harry: When I grow up I'm going to marry Grandpa.
Mum: I'm afraid you can't do that, Harry.
Harry: Why not?
Mum: Because he's my father.
Harry: Well, you married my father!

Joe: You're never going to die, are you Grandma?
Gran: (*Gently breaking the bad news.*) Well, I might have to some day, you know, Joe.
Joe: Oh well, could you do it when I'm at school?

Gran: (*Showing granddaughter photo of herself at twenty*) Who do you think that is, Anna?
Anna: Don't know.
Gran: (*Disappointed*) It's me when I was young.
Anna: You're still young, Gran.

I love my Gran and Grandpa because they are nice and soft to cuddle, and Gran has holes in her ears, and Grandpa has hairs in his nose and they sleep a lot.

My bed is beside my Grandad's and he holds my hand while I go to sleep.

When we arrive at my Nan's house, she always says,
'Mercy, it's the invasion!'

Park there, Grandpa. Look, no bloody yellow lines.

Nan, I dreamt that you were flying about in the air, holding
a cup of tea.

Grandpa: Why are you crying, Tom?
Tom: I'm sad for my baby sister.
Grandpa: Why?
Tom: 'Cos she's bald like you, Grandpa, and she's a girl!

It was said of the novelist, Sir Hugh Walpole, that he did not speak at all until he was three and a half years old, by which time his family had almost given up hope and feared for his mental capabilities. One day, his grandmother accidentally scalded him on the hand whilst pouring tea. The boy was brave about it but was obviously in some pain. After a time his grandmother asked him if he was feeling any better. Out came little Hugh's first words ever ... 'Thank you, Grandmama, the agony has somewhat abated.'

Contents

Introduction

How did this book come to be written? I suppose it was the result of a rare lunch I enjoyed with my daughter about a year ago. I say rare because, since she became a mother, the number of times we have been able to lunch alone together can be counted on one finger. Anyway, during our meal we were discussing (and laughing about) our unusual family, when it dawned on us that it might not be all that unusual – that, in fact, it is fairly representative of late 20th-century trends.

We seem to cover all possible modern scenarios. I am a grandmother, divorced from my first husband (now deceased) and remarried to a second husband, Paul, who is therefore a stepgrandfather. Paul is also divorced, with one daughter from an early relationship, one adopted daughter from his first marriage, and one stepdaughter, Peggy, from his second marriage to me. Complicated, isn't it?

I shall never forget the devastating moment when I told Peggy that I had fallen in love with Paul and that he was coming to live with us. She looked at me with all the world-weariness of 12 years spent with a mad actress mother and said, 'You know,

Mum, sometimes I wonder if I can take much more of you.' Luckily for me and for Paul, she could and did!

Peggy is married to a British-born Sikh, Dharminder, so we have mixed-race grandchildren. Our grandson, Sky, is four years old, and our granddaughter, Biba, is two. Peggy and Dharminder both work, so although Peggy is based at home, she has help with the children. Paul and I are actors – writing, directing and teaching as well – so we also work full-time and, typically for modern grandparents, don't live around the corner from our grandchildren, but a two-hour drive away: Peggy and Dharminder are in London while we are near Stratford-on-Avon. The children's paternal grandmother, a widow, also lives two hours away from them, in Leicester.

So there you have it. As people who might be described as 'modern' grandparents, we decided to try to write an up-to-the-minute account of how our new role has changed and enriched our lives and, indeed, how we manage to juggle our various commitments.

That was how the idea began. After that, as word spread about the book, so many people made contact and expressed an interest that we realized that the book might become more than just a personal account. Potentially, it could also reflect the views and experiences of many other families – both nuclear and fragmented as our own. When my husband and I travelled to the United States on tour with *Henry VIII* (now there's a complicated family man for you!) all kinds of American family experiences were recounted to us too.

I have been constantly delighted by people's enthusiastic reaction to our subject. Far from having to coax information and opinions out of them, grandparents, parents and grandchildren alike have been delighted to share experiences and pour out confidences. So much so that, in the end, I found I had amassed enough material for several novels!

There seems to be a widespread resurgence of interest in the whole question of grandparenting. After a partial eclipse, the importance of the relationship is assuming its rightful place in the general consciousness. Recently, the novelist and grandparent Alice Thomas Ellis wrote (in The *Times*, 26th September 1998):

> *Social engineering has interfered with natural processes and often grandma lives far from the family and cannot assist on a daily basis. A surprising number of young women seem to regret this. Having grown out of the rebellious teenage stage they find they want their mothers ... New man has not quite lived up to expectations ...*

This article was written in response to a new theory of evolution, hot from Dr Kristen Hawks of the University of Utah, which asserts that man's biological success in becoming a larger-brained species was entirely thanks to grandparents:

> *Grannies were able to forage for roots and vegetables which they could give to their daughters when they were having babies, creating a well-nourished, thriving third generation ... Grannies became so important that the menopause evolved to stop them having children of their own late in life.*

Apparently, we are the only species in which the female has a menopause, which allows her to become a good, foraging granny!

Well, we may no longer be in charge of grubbing for roots and vegetables, but there are still many other ways in which grannies, and grandfathers too, can help – as we have tried to suggest in this book – to create a thriving third generation.

We hope you get as much fun and pleasure from being grandparents as we do.

Chapter 1

I Can't Be a Grandparent

The Announcement

'Mum? Listen! I'm pregnant. You're going to be grandparents!'

No matter how often you may have anticipated this news and even longed for it to come, no one can be prepared for the wave of emotion that hits you upon actually hearing it. I remember clearly the moment of my daughter's phone call – the joy, excitement, relief and slight apprehension; the feeling of being about to step into a new role, and the awareness that my genes were being carried on into the future. I remember shouting to my husband, 'You're going to be a Grandpa,' and his rather startled expression.

Dozens of thoughts raced around my mind at once, because nothing can prepare you for the peculiar mixture of emotions you feel when you hear the big news. Of course, some of you will already know what I'm talking about. Questions come tumbling out: 'When is it due? How do you feel? When did you find out? How does X feel about it? (The partner, if involved.) Have you got morning sickness? Have you told anyone else yet?'

And the unspoken questions: 'Have you any idea of just how much your lives are about to change? How on earth are you going to manage in that little flat? What'll happen when you've only got one lot of money coming in?' There is sometimes even a little selfish demon muttering things like, 'But I'm too young!' 'I'm not ready to be a grandparent yet!' 'What about my busy schedule?'

Peggy Writes

Telling Mum and Paul was probably the most exciting moment of the pregnancy. After my husband, they were the first to know. It was only in telling them that I really believed it myself. Before that, it was as if I had made it up – it just didn't seem possible. I had done four tests, as the first was very faint, and although they were all positive I wondered whether they were wrong. When I told them this, they laughed and reassured me – which, in a way, has been their role ever since.

Reactions

Reactions to the big news vary in the extreme. Rather like the parents themselves, the grandparents-to-be may shuttle backwards and forwards between excitement and apprehension. One young woman's mother and father arrived on her doorstep the day after they'd heard, bearing armfuls of flowers and champagne: 'I couldn't drink the champagne, of course, but I needn't have worried, they had the lot! But I just couldn't believe how thrilled they were. They'd taken a plane from Scotland especially. Their happiness took away any slight misgivings we may have had and convinced us we'd done the right thing.'

Another was not so lucky: 'The first thing my mother said to me on hearing the news was, "Well, I hope you don't expect me to look after it for you." I was shattered. I had phoned her full of excitement and so happy and she burst my balloon. I felt as if she had slapped me over the face. I cried my eyes out when I got off the phone.'

One grandmother (in the book *Grandmothers Talking to Nell Dunn*) said, 'I think the real function of grandparents is to support the parents – above all.' A wise remark – and this support cannot start too soon, right from the moment you hear the news. If, by any chance, you have any misgivings, now is not the time to express them. Just keep right in there behind the parent, or parents as the case may be. After all, they've usually got enough anxieties without our adding to them.

'My first reaction was very mixed because my son wasn't married to his girlfriend at the time. I told him they should tie the knot right away, but he said he didn't want anyone to think it was a shotgun wedding. Also, I suppose, because they weren't married, I had never thought of myself as a grandmother before. It was a bit of a shock.'

It's a good idea to vocalize your support, be it practical or financial, or both. There's nothing more reassuring to a young couple starting out on that biggest rite of passage than to know that they have some help to fall back on. And, of course, this is all the more so in the case of a single mother. No pregnant woman bravely facing bringing up a child alone needs to hear anything negative.

4

'For 11 years my daughter had told me that I would never be a grandmother because the doctors had pronounced her infertile. So of course I was utterly delighted, really over the moon, because I never expected it. And they decided to get married too. I said to them, "Don't get married for my sake," but they insisted they wanted to anyway. No, really, apart from having my own child, I couldn't have felt more pleased about anything. Well, I was ready for it. I didn't want to be too old a Grandma. I am 65.'

'When I Had You'

Another area in which grandparents (all right, perhaps more usually grand*mothers*) can be supportive is in being open-minded about healthcare choices during pregnancy and the parents' plans for the birth. These can sometimes seem very bizarre to our generation, but as will be explained in more detail later, pregnancy care and birth practices have changed beyond belief over the past 20, not to say 30, years. So if you don't know what she is talking about when it comes to folic acid or toxoplasmosis, ask her what they mean, and don't pooh-pooh things you don't know about yet. I say this from experience because I was quite a sceptic until I knew better!

Help! What Does It Mean?

Active Birth: Coined by the famous pioneer of natural childbirth, Janet Balaskas, this term describes labours in which the mother remains mobile, with complete freedom of movement. She may choose to walk about, to squat, to kneel or to lean on her birth partner. Of course, she may also lie down, but only if it is her choice to do so. This body-centred approach encourages the mother to have faith in the natural process of birth and to use breathing, meditation, massage and water for pain relief. The International Active Birth Movement promotes this approach worldwide and is based at the Active Birth Centre in London.

Water Birth: The therapeutic properties of water have been known about for thousands of years and women have always used water as a relaxant – think of how having a bath helped the cramps of period pains. Today, at long last, water is recognized as a highly effective form of pain relief for labour and birth. Whether the mother simply showers or gets in the bath, or whether she uses a purpose-designed birth pool, the effect is similar. The benefit of a pool, however, is that the woman has more mobility in it and can stay in it comfortably for hours. Most women choose to come out for the actual birth, and some to stay in – often they don't know exactly what they will decide to do until the time comes. Babies born under water don't take their first breath until they are brought up to the surface, but if you are worried about what might seem like a danger, then

> – rather than battle with the mother over the issue – resist commenting until you know more. Buy a book on the subject, read up, and if you are still concerned, talk to the obstetrician (with the mother's permission).

It's very important, too, not to indulge in any scare stories. No matter what a hard time you had giving birth, no daughter or daughter-in-law wants to hear about it. Nor son-in-law for that matter. I know my own mother scared the life out of me by telling me that she was dreading my labour because she'd had three difficult births – 'They were AGONY, darling!' – and that as I was as narrow-hipped as she was, so she feared for a similar experience. In the event, her dire prophecies proved quite unfounded and she could have saved me quite a lot of apprehension had she kept her misgivings to herself. I know it was because she genuinely didn't want me to suffer, but there is no need to anticipate something that may never happen.

Your New Status

Everyone needs to have access both to grandparents and grandchildren in order to be a full human being.

Margaret Mead

Grandparents can have a huge and lasting influence in the life of the coming child. Just think how seldom you hear people bad-mouthing grandparents compared to the general berating of poor parents that goes on! Indeed, grandparents are often remembered with intense love and respect – a respect not always consciously incurred.

Paul Writes

I loved my grandfather. He would sit in his chair and spit in the fire. It used to sizzle on the coal. He'd put clouds of grey pepper over his chips, then leave most of them. I hated pepper so I couldn't eat any. But he always had time to play with me.

It does seem to be true that alone with their grandparents, children relax, perhaps because they are not as emotionally involved with them as with their parents. Also, most grandparents have this great plus – novelty value! In many cases, Grandma and Grandad arrive, have a great time spoiling their grandchildren and then disappear again. Or the grandchild comes for a lovely and special visit. The poor parents stand little chance of competing with this when they've got to do all the day-to-day care and disciplining that goes with parenting.

So when you get the big news you can bask in dreams of how much fun you're going to have and how popular you are going to be. Never mind all these wet wipes and tissues you're going to have to start carrying about your person.

Ageing Worries – and How to Lose Them

Paul Writes

As a step-Grandpa-to-be, when I heard the news I naturally didn't experience any feeling of pride that my own genes were being carried on. However, somehow that didn't in the least diminish my excitement and joy. I felt elated, but at the same time hoped I'd make the grade as a grandparent, as I felt I was quite young and immature myself. And, yes, I suppose – if I'm being very honest – there was a bit of panic at the idea of becoming that venerable being, a grandfather.

There's no doubt about it, getting used to the idea of being a grandparent requires quite a big shift in one's thinking. As Sheila Kitzinger says, 'It is a rite of passage which is not made nearly such a fuss of as motherhood, quite rightly, as it is not *such* an enormous life change, but still it is a life change and as such has not been greatly acknowledged.'

Interestingly enough, from the cross-section of people I have talked to for this book, it seems to be men who have most difficulty in adapting to the idea of being that archetypal figure connected with old age: a grandparent. One man was startlingly honest: 'I was horrified. I didn't like the idea of being a grandfather at all. It put an image into my mind of old people and I don't feel old at all inside.'

I had thought it might be women who would have more trouble with moving into the third generation. I suppose I was unconsciously accepting the tendency of ageism to focus on women (all those little-old-lady stereotypes of grandmothers knitting in rocking chairs). Possibly women are just cleverer about hiding their fears about it, but they genuinely seem more easy in the role than men. As one woman said, 'When my first grandchild was born, I lost my fear of ageing. Everything seemed to fall into place. Besides, she sits on my knee and says, "I love your lines, Grandma."'

Perhaps this acceptance is also made easier for women because, in spite of all the 'Glamorous Grannies' around, many are not as sexually active as they once were. Older men, on the other hand, are often still considered to be contestants in the sexual arena. Even if they don't want to play! If, in front of a younger woman, a man says, 'my grandchild', it immediately places him in an age bracket to which he may not wish to belong, especially if he looks younger than he is.

For some women, however, difficulties arise when they are either still fertile themselves or newly menopausal. A friend admitted that when she heard the news, she was ashamed to feel rather envious of her daughter's fecundity and that she immediately had the desire to become pregnant. (This impulse may partly explain the number of nieces and nephews who are older than their aunts and uncles.)

As women, one of the hardest facts we have to face up to is our loss of fertility at quite an early age in comparison with men. All I can say to comfort any grandmother-to-be with faint yearnings in this direction is that these feelings are usually extinguished by the birth of the grandchild, when you can re-experience almost all your maternal delights without the sleeplessness and anxiety that went with them the first time around.

As for all you young-looking grandmothers and grandfathers-to-be, you can look forward to astonished faces and flattering remarks: 'You can't be a grandparent – it's impossible!'

R.U.S.C!

After receiving the news, try to remember that you still have several months in which to psyche yourself to become R.U.S.C! – RELIABLE, UNCRITICAL, SUPPORTIVE and CALM. Practise the skill of biting your tongue before offering a suggestion, unless you are appealed to directly for your opinion – and even then think carefully before replying. Above all, prepare yourself for any ideas you might come up with to be rejected as old-fashioned and completely ridiculous. Learn to smile in a jolly way when you are made fun of. Try to remember what you were like yourself as a young mother or father, and how you felt when your parents or parents-in-law made what seemed to you utterly unsuitable suggestions. Acknowledge to yourself that things keep moving on, especially ideas on childcare. Remember even the late, great Dr Spock was somewhat discredited in the end – especially by himself!

A fine method of whiling away the time before the birth is to find out which childcare books (if any) the parents-to-be are reading and read them yourself. A great deal of potential conflict can be avoided if this is done. You may not entirely agree with every new idea, but at least you will have an informed opinion – and more insight into what has contributed to their choices. Much better to discuss calmly the various methods and theories *before* the birth, than to argue and criticize later when the young parents are struggling to do their best as they see it. An intelligent mind is an open mind, and that has nothing to do with age.

Celebrate!

For the moment, just think of the fun you can have rushing around telling everyone that you're expecting your first grandchild and observing their reactions. Not everyone will be interested; some may even look at you with a pitying expression ('Poor old thing, you really *are* past it'), but good friends will share your delight, especially those who already have grandchildren themselves. So, if you are among the lucky ones who have just received the big news, go out and celebrate. You are about to move on to a new and wonderful time of your lives!

Chapter 2

Only 230 Knitting Days

The Pregnancy and Birth

So, you've come to terms with the idea of the pregnancy, and excitement begins to grow along with the bump. But, oh, how long it seems to take! What can you do to be most helpful? Again, this very much depends on individual situations. Is the mother-to-be on her own? Do you live near? Is she having an easy pregnancy? It's very often a play-it-by-ear scenario, but probably the best thing anyone can do is to let it be known that they are available if needed, even if it's just for reassuring chats on the phone. Keep as closely in touch as possible, without seeming to be constantly checking, which can be rather irritating – as one young woman found:

'My mother-in-law kept phoning me on an almost daily basis, closely questioning me as to all my symptoms: what I was eating, was I getting enough rest, and didn't I think I should give up work sooner than the time I had planned to take my maternity leave. It drove me mad. It was like a take-over bid. Eventually I got so incensed that I said to her one day, "My own mother doesn't ask me all these questions." That really put the cat among the pigeons. She went into a right huff and I hardly heard from her again until after the baby was born. Bit of a relief, really. But I felt badly about it. After all, she was only trying to help. But everything's all right between us now and she's actually a super grandma.'

Many pregnant women welcome help with housework or shopping, especially in the later months of pregnancy, when it can be bliss to have an afternoon nap while somebody else copes. Make sure that any food you might provide at this time is healthy and safe (i.e. no rare beef or soft cheese, etc.), and encourage the pregnant mother to eat a balanced and healthy diet. During my daughter's first pregnancy, my general knowledge about diet and health improved immensely, and it made me wonder how on earth I had managed when I was expecting her and was in a state of ignorance about the healthiest options.

Lots of women of my generation acknowledge that they didn't know the first thing about healthcare when they were carrying their children, and some share feelings of guilt about that unawareness. One grandmother-to-be admitted that she secretly read up on contemporary childcare because she knew she was going to stay with her daughter for the first two weeks after the birth and she didn't want to show how much she didn't know or had forgotten.

Others say that they didn't read any childcare books then and they're not going to start now. They maintain that a woman 'knows these things by instinct' and insist that 'young mums read far too many of these books nowadays'. While I do not entirely agree with them, there is no doubt that Mother Nature *does* often step in when needed.

When I was young I drank and smoked, not to excess, but more than I should have. As soon as I was pregnant I was unable to do either. Even the idea of a drink made me feel sick, and a smoky atmosphere was unbearable. As for coffee, I had to cross the street to avoid the *smell* from a coffee shop or café, far less drink any. No one really discussed pregnancy then (I'm talking about the early sixties) let alone gave you advice about it. I remember playing Alison in John Osborne's *Look Back in Anger* and when it came to her line, 'You see, I'm pregnant ...' there was an audible gasp from the audience. No one said that word then except doctors. It was all euphemisms: 'She's in the family way.' 'She's expecting a happy event,' or in vulgar parlance, 'She's got a bun in the oven.' There were no proper antenatal classes, and you were still expected to draw as little attention to your condition as possible. I was recording a television series at the time, and I had to keep rushing out to be secretly sick in the ladies' room. I pretended I had an upset stomach, as I was afraid that if I made my condition known too early, they'd give my part to someone else (which they probably would have done).

I would love to have had the knowledge that young women have today. Not all of them follow the guidelines, but most do and have healthier, happier babies as a result. It is wonderful to realize just how woman-centred pregnancy and birth care has become, thanks greatly to the work of The National Childbirth Trust in Britain, but also to women themselves. Many in my generation do indeed look back in anger to the way we were treated when doctors 'knew best' and we did as we were told.

Women were often forced out of control of their own bodies, and giving birth was too often medicalized to such a degree that to make any individual request was considered being 'difficult'. Pethidine was frequently administered without our asking for it, with a resulting loss of mental alertness in the mother, and the potential problem of its affecting the baby. Although I'm sure this was done in an attempt to relieve any suffering, it was not always ascertained – and certainly not in my case – that any real suffering had begun. This description, from *Mother and Baby*, June 1965, suggests just how clinical birthing had become. Pregnant women were told:

> At the beginning of the second stage you will be taken to the labour room ... This is a small, bare room with a high bed in it where your baby will be born in aseptic conditions. The doctor and midwife will don masks just as for a surgical operation ... The obstetric bed is steel-based and provides good support for you in the pushing stage. You will be placed on your back, thighs wide apart and your legs up in the air, supported by two leather stirrups. This is called the lithotomy position and is used to enable whoever is delivering you to control the descent of your baby's head through the birth canal. You will, of course, be draped in sterile towels and you will find the position quite suitable for the hard work you have to do.

Tests and Scans

Most expectant mothers do not need to be encouraged to have all the tests and scans that may be necessary. In fact, it's sometimes older people who think there may be too many of these, and that they might cause too much stress. Most, however, find them as reassuring as the parents do. A friend of mine who is just about to become a grandmother phoned me recently thrilled to bits because she had just been to her daughter's scan with her. 'I was really touched that she wanted me to go with her,' she said. 'Isn't it wonderful, and doesn't it make you realize how little information there was available to us when we had our babies. Parents are so lucky these days.'

One of the great bi-products of working on this book is that I get unexpected phone calls from grandparents, potential grandparents and parents themselves who offer interesting facts and stories, and ask me about some comparable circumstances.

Sometimes grandparents-to-be say that to them a scan looks like a map of the dark side of the moon and they can recognize nothing even vaguely resembling a baby. Don't be afraid to ask for it to be explained to you, and then you can share the thrill.

Another friend of mine, whose daughter had to have a late scan, said, 'We didn't particularly want to know the sex of the child but on the picture it was quite obvious that it was a boy. Impossible to ignore that little thing waving about in the breeze.'

Parents may or may not choose to have scans and tests – the decision must be theirs – but those who do can find these procedures reassuring. So much of the pregnancy experience used to be a guessing game, with pregnant women too often at the mercy of old wives' horror stories.

A Little Knowledge is a Dangerous Thing!

'My father was a GP with a busy practice in Glasgow. I was living in London and pregnant with my first child. My husband wasn't particularly interested in any of my symptoms and I was far away from close female friends. Also, I idolized my father and I valued his medical opinion highly. So every day, at least once, I used to phone him.

'I knew he really loved me so it never occurred to me that I could be being a bit of a pest when I used to phone him in the middle of his consulting hours with the latest symptom. What did so-and-so mean? Should I eat such-and-such? Why was I feeling this, that and the other? During the whole nine months he would patiently explain every tiniest detail to me. My phone bill rocketed and so, I'm sure, did his, as if he was unavailable I would leave messages for him to phone me back. Eventually, on the day before my daughter was born, I went to the loo and found I had a show of a jelly-like substance. (This turned out to be the stopper of the womb and meant that birth was pretty imminent.) Immediately, I went into overdrive and phoned Glasgow: "Dad, what does it mean, this jelly?" There was a long pause. Then my father's voice said dryly, "Well, dear, I expect it means you're going to have a Jelly Baby." Even a saint's patience can run out!'

Names

Try to be magnanimous when the parents-to-be tell you their latest great idea for a name. Remember you can get used to anything. But it's probably all right to point out any potentially tease-worthy names: for instance, if their surname is Button and they propose to call a daughter Pearl. I have known a girl called Dawn Pink and a boy called Rock Salmon. In both cases, I think it was the mother or father's idea of a witticism. Not very fair on the kids, though. Schoolchildren can turn even potentially harmless names into something deadly, so it pays to be careful, even with initials –

M T Head is *not* such a good idea. One of the reasons my parents called me Claire was because they considered it a name that could not be shortened or easily corrupted into a nickname. They reckoned without the school wit who dubbed me 'Chocolate éclair'.

Often parents will appeal to the grandparents for ideas, so have a few names ready just in case they do. But try not to sulk if they don't even consider them!

Hasn't She Had It Yet?

The grandparents usually find that, as the due date grows ever nearer, and the mother-to-be gets ever larger, there is more they can do to help. The last few weeks can seem to last a lifetime for the expectant mother, when every movement is an effort. So it is a time when even the smallest offering, like giving her a back-rub or cooking a meal, can be very much appreciated. Also, this is a good time to encourage the parents-to-be to go out together, because it is probably going to be a long while before they will be able to go out alone again.

You may find yourself getting almost as impatient for the event as the couple, especially as neighbours and friends seem to keep asking that old question, 'Hasn't she had it yet?' I remember feeling quite nostalgic in advance for the times by ourselves that my daughter and I had shared, because I knew that they could never return. But then I shook myself and thought, no those times can't, but the new ones can be even better!

Paul Writes

I found it extremely touching to witness Peggy's pregnancy advancing. She is one of those young women who blooms, looks radiant, and seems to sail through the whole thing with aplomb. She was also very busy nest-building, making a whole new flat perfect for the coming baby, in the perfectionist way she does everything. Sometimes, secretly, I felt just a little sad. I don't know why. I can only think that it was something to do with her growing up completely, or a sense of a new era approaching (or maybe a realization of my own ageing) – I'm not sure. Also, Claire had once miscarried a child that we had longed for, and I suppose that, because my wife is rather like her daughter, it made me think of what it would have been like if she had carried the baby to term. Towards the end of Peggy's pregnancy, we were very excited and full of curiosity about the coming child – though finally you just think, 'Come on, baby, will you!'

The Birth

This is an exciting but often rather disturbing time for grandparents-to-be because usually there is nothing you can do but wait … and wait … and wait. Trying to hide any anxiety, wanting to help without being able to, feeling utterly impotent and slightly apprehensive at the same time is not much fun. Many women report a sense of total inadequacy and seem to share a primitive urge to be at the actual birth, perhaps because in the collective memory birth may often have been an all-female affair, as it is to this day in some communities.

I was extremely interested to read a book about southeast Asian birth customs, which was written in 1965, a time when birth in the Western world was extremely clinical, men were discouraged to be present, and women were placed on their backs, with their legs in stirrups. In contrast, Asian customs of the time quite closely resembled many of our so-called 'modern' birthing practices. This is about the Caticugan people:

> The husband's presence is essential to perform certain tasks: his absence angers the spirits.

A woman's husband may assist the midwife if the delivery is complicated. Some Caticugan women cling to their husbands, who encourage them to exert greater effort during labour.

Massage is a therapeutic treatment closely associated with the traditional management of pregnancy and delivery in the Philippines.

During labour massage is often used to hasten a dilatory foetus. The woman may also stand and then squat to facilitate birth.

South East Asian Birth Customs, Dinn. V. Hart, Phya Anuman Rajadhon and Richard J. Coughlin

Everything comes full circle it seems!

Birth Partners

It may still happen that a woman wants her mother present, especially if she is single, but usually – and quite naturally – it is her partner she will choose to help her give birth.

Heidi: 'I was terribly hurt when my son said, "Don't come to the hospital, Mum." And "We'd rather you weren't there when we bring the baby home." It was only later that he told me he had said this because he felt concern that, due to the fact that his mother-in-law had recently died, it would make his wife sad if *his* mother were too much in evidence. In the event I did get to see my new grandson in hospital, born eight days early, but a fine big baby, and they were happy for me to be at the house, where I had everything clean and ready and a meal cooked, when they brought him home.'

Marge: 'My husband went to bed but I stayed up sipping brandy and milk, with my son-in-law ringing me from the hospital in London every so often. It's a drink I've never drunk before or since! I think I needed it because the birth was not easy. I felt helpless and yes, I did wish I could be there, though in a cowardly way I was glad I wasn't. I wouldn't have liked to see my daughter suffering. The baby got stuck and she ended up having to have a Caesarean. I was utterly delighted when I heard it was a boy. I hadn't made up my mind but that's what I hoped it would be. Why? I like men.'

Pam: 'When my first grandchild was born, although it was April, there was such thick snow that I couldn't get to the hospital to see him. I felt terrible about that. It made me remember that exactly the same thing happened when I had my first child. There was an April blizzard and my mother couldn't get up from Wales to visit us.'

Sophie: 'Although my daughter had no real difficulties, the actual birth was a real trauma for me. I felt *awful*. I would rather have been having the baby myself, I felt so useless and helpless. I was completely uptight and I had no one to share it with, being on my own.'

Kay: 'I was with my daughter during it all and she was fantastic! She never made a sound. Only when the doctor said, "One more push, Sally, one more push." Then she gave a sort of long squeal, and there was my granddaughter! I had arranged for music to be played: *Canon in D* by Johann Pachelbel. The nurse loved it so much she wanted to know what it was. She said she would play it for other mothers giving birth because it's so soothing.'

Joan: 'The actual birth was a terrible, horrible time for us. We knew that she had gone into hospital, that she was in labour, but time went on and time went on and there was no word. I kept phoning the hospital but they just told me, "No, there's no news yet" and were generally very cagey. Eventually we went to bed, but of course I couldn't sleep. Early in the morning I phoned and they said, "Yes, your daughter has had her baby." I said, "Is she all right?" and they said she was. I was so relieved it was only afterwards that I realized I had forgotten to ask whether it was a boy or a girl! At last my son-in-law rang to say, "We have a baby daughter. Can you both come to the hospital now – we're shattered." We were delighted to go. I had felt so totally helpless that it was a relief to be able to do something. Yes, I would have loved to have been with my daughter but I felt it was not my place.'

Martin: 'Although I was excited and full of anticipation, I must admit I did feel an awful sense of strain whilst my daughter was giving birth, and tremendous relief when it was over. To be there was the last thing on earth I would have wanted. I could never stand it when she was little and skinned her knees. That broke me up enough. I couldn't bear seeing her suffer if I couldn't take the pain away. But we older men weren't allowed anywhere near our wives when they were having babies and I can't help feeling we missed out.'

Peggy Writes

I knew that Mum wanted to be with me during the birth, and felt very guilty about excluding her. I think I'd also want to be with my daughter, and can quite understand the impulse. But I just felt that I might not be able to do it with her there. Firstly, there is the privacy issue – we have never been a family to walk about the house naked. But more important than this was my concern that, were she there, I would feel like a daughter, and not like a mother myself. My Mum is very, very sympathetic and nurturing, and I worried that her concern would weaken me. My husband, on the other had, is extremely pragmatic. With him there, I felt I'd just have to get on with it – which I did!

So … the big event is over. To everyone's joy and excitement, the baby has arrived. You hurry to the hospital and gaze upon the new infant. Don't worry too much if you don't feel deep affection for him or her at once. I found, from talking to others, that what happened to my husband and me is very common. Though you are proud and happy, you feel at first a little shy of the baby, of this little stranger who has arrived in your lives. Often there isn't the immediate bonding that happens with your own child. But then, quite suddenly – sometimes sooner, sometimes later, but always when you are least expecting it – you fall helplessly and head-over-heels in love with your grandchild. You are utterly besotted and in a state of infatuation which, happily, will last for as long as you live!

Chapter 3

Rather You
Than Me

The Immediate Postnatal Period

Now you can really come into your own as grandparents, if time and circumstances allow. I have often thought that not only should the father have compassionate leave, but perhaps one or other of the grandparents as well! As Dr Christopher Green wisely says, 'Grandmas and grandpas are some of the most valuable, and least utilised natural resources.'

The immediate postnatal period is perhaps the most stressful of all for new parents, especially for the mother because her hormones can be very unsettled after the birth. I remember sitting in the car going home from the hospital with my new baby on my knee (yes, it was before the days of baby seats – or even safety belts for that matter; I don't know how any of us survived!) and completely panicking: I CAN'T DO THIS! I DON'T KNOW HOW! I'VE NEVER BEEN A PARENT BEFORE! HELP!

So for grandparents who are within call this is an ideal time to help, especially by responding to requests. Please don't make the mistake many do of assuming that you *must* leave them and not interfere – that it's a time for them to get to know their baby and bond as a new family. It may be that they want to be left alone, but do *make sure*. I've often heard such wails as: 'Oh, if only our parents had helped us in the first two or three weeks. We felt so alone. I hadn't got my full strength back and he (the partner) was *so* irritable all the time. We just kept quarrelling about what was the right thing to do' and 'I did wish her Mum had popped round more often. We could have done with catching up on some sleep just at the beginning.'

It is obviously easier for grandparents to offer help to a single parent because they can feel pretty sure of being needed and there's no danger of irritating their son or daughter's partner. In fact, just because there are two parents doesn't mean that the partner may not also welcome a bit of help. In the lucky but unusual case of two sets of grandparents being available, then co-operation between them can divide the load, prevent any feeling of being left out, and make for closeness between the older couples. Looking after new infants is tiring enough for young parents, but is especially so for those not in the first flush of youth. One new mother commented that the best thing her mother and mother-in-law did was to come round alternately every day to let her go to bed for a couple of hours. Sleep deprivation is a serious strain on new parents and not to be underestimated, so any help that allows them to catch up on some rest can be invaluable.

For the new parents this baby is the be-all and end-all of their world, so it is important for them to feel that, in spite of your busy and active life, you are prepared to shelve anything that's possible in order to lend them a hand. It may not appear particularly relevant to them if you refuse a plea for help because you have to go to a party! A reasonable degree of self-sacrifice is necessary at this crucial time. Help may also be welcome with the chores that need to be done for the sake of good hygiene, but mean time spent away from their baby – like washing the kitchen floor, cleaning the loo or clearing out the fridge. If, physically, you are not up to these tasks, just sitting there holding the baby and lending a sympathetic ear can be just as helpful.

Again, as with anything else, don't be afraid to *ask* what the parents might like to have done for them. This way they won't feel that you're trying to 'take over'. It's best to establish right from the beginning that you will tell them honestly if it is impossible for you to come at any particular time. That way they won't be afraid to make requests and will be less likely to take offence if you can't oblige. To start with too high a level of assistance, which you cannot sustain, can cause misunderstandings and disappointment on both sides. Honesty is undoubtedly the best policy.

Top 10 Gifts for Young Babies

It can be quite irritating for parents to be given 25 teddies for their newborn when so many useful and stimulating toys are now available for young babies. Of course, you'll want to buy things, but it's probably a good idea to check with the parents first to see what they have already bought or been given. I know one proud grandmother who turned up with a large, expensive baby bouncer, only to find that the parents had just been out to buy one exactly the same. You might consider buying:

- A baby gym – an activity frame that you put over the baby as it lies on its back
- A mobile: preferably a 'Stim Mobile' with bold black-and-white graphics that the young baby's eyes can easily see
- A musical light show: a wind-up 'son et lumière' that projects a moving display of pictures on the ceiling or wall to the accompaniment of soothing music
- Books or cards with stimulating bright geometric patterns: newborns can focus more easily on patterns with marked contrasts and are usually fascinated by them
- A wobble globe: a kind of rattle on a sucker that can be fixed to flat surfaces and is a great distraction during nappy changes

- A sound and texture toy: for instance, the octopuses/snakes that are made out of variously textured materials, and make different noises: rattles, squeaks, etc.
- Jack-in-the-box: from birth babies love 'now you see it, now you don't' toys
- Stacking cups: a classic and inexpensive toy that will be played with throughout babyhood
- Activity mat: a soft, brightly coloured mat boasting a range of attractions for babies – from mirrors to dials and flaps
- Activity centre: a similar multi-activity toy that encourages the baby to press, pull, look and listen

'My mother was a nightmare just after Elly was born. She kept coming round with friends and neighbours for them "just to take a little peek at my grandchild". She never seemed to think that it might be an awkward time or that there were other things that needed to be done. They'd stay for hours and I'd end up having to make tea for them all and falling behind with everything else. If it hadn't been for Roy's dad, I think I'd have gone mad. He was really helpful. He did my shopping all the time, brought us in takeaways and he even changed Ellie's nappies once or twice. I told him that he really is a New Man!'

Breastfeeding – the Big Issue!

Try to be as supportive as possible of the mother's breast-feeding. Recent research has shown that 'breast is best', offering an instant, perfectly balanced diet for the new baby, which enhances the infant's immune system and seems also to decrease the chances of the child developing allergies and certain other illnesses in later life. It can also strengthen the mother-child relationship and seems to give enormous satisfaction to the baby, who may find instant and reliable comfort from the breast.

But breastfeeding isn't always easy at first. The baby may seem to refuse the breast, have difficulty 'latching-on' properly, or nipple suck, causing pain and distress to the mother. If this is the case, rather than try to dissuade her from continuing, you might suggest that she ask the nurse, midwife or health visitor to advise her on positioning the baby correctly at the breast, changing breasts and other such helpful solutions. If you breastfed, you may be able to offer this advice yourself; but if you didn't, the kindest thing you can do is to support and encourage her, rather than make her feel that she has in some way failed. Breastfeeding is a very emotive issue, and the feeling that she cannot feed her baby can deeply disturb a mother and knock her confidence.

Of course there are women who may not be able to or do not wish to breastfeed. The choice must lie with the mother. It is her body and only she can decide what is possible and practicable for her.

So whatever route she chooses – breastfeeding or bottle-feeding, it is best to be as positive as possible to the parents and be careful not to increase any anxieties that they may have. After all, lots of healthy, happy and strapping people were reared on the bottle (and I don't mean gin!) and lots on the breast. Remember the old saying:

And still the baby thrives and grows, and how it does, God only knows!

Bottle-feeding – the Routine

Even if you did it with your own children, bottle-feeding can be rather daunting. The sterilizing, the mixing, the warming – it can all be too much like a science exam (with the parents as invigilators!). But, happily, it needn't be like this. Once you are in the routine, it will be as easy as riding the proverbial bicycle. Wash your hands thoroughly, then:

1 **WASH THE BOTTLES AND TEATS**
   Use hot water and detergent in a clean washing-up bowl. With a bottlebrush, wash the bottles, teats, discs, rings and caps inside and out to remove all traces of milk, not forgetting rims and crevasses (force water through the holes in the teats). Now rinse the bottle parts under a cold mains tap.

2 **STERILIZE THE BOTTLES AND TEATS BY ONE OF THE FOLLOWING METHODS:**
   Boiling: immerse the bottle parts in a pan of boiling water, cover and simmer for 10 minutes. Then either fish them out on to a plate rinsed in hot water or leave them to cool in the water, keeping the pan covered, and use when required.
   Steaming: use a purpose-designed electric steam sterilizer according to the manufacturer's instructions.
   Microwaving: use a purpose-designed microwave sterilizer, again according to the manufacturer's instructions.
   Chemical sterilization: immerse bottles and teats in a plastic container containing the appropriate mixture of

water and sterilization chemicals (either in tablet or liquid form). Rinse with boiled, cooled water before use.

3 **MAKE UP THE FEED**

Thoroughly wash and dry your hands. Read the instructions on the milk extremely carefully and follow them to the letter. Pour into the bottle (or bottles – you can make enough for one day's feeding and keep them in the fridge if you like) the recommended amount of boiled, cooled water. Now, with a well-washed and rinsed scoop (filled so as to be level), add the appropriate amount of milk powder. Put the bottle together with the cap firmly on and shake vigorously until the milk has a smooth, even consistency.

4 **WARM THE FEED**

It's best to warm the feed the old-fashioned way, in a bowl of warm water, rather than in a microwave, which can heat unevenly; then check the temperature by dropping a little milk on to your wrist. When the drops feel slightly warm, it's ready for the baby. (If you are in a hurry, and do resort to the microwave, shake the heated bottle very well to mix in any hot spots and never forget to check the temperature of the milk before feeding.)

5 **FEED!**

With the baby in the crook of your arm, give the bottle for as long as she seems happy sucking. But keep watching (and don't go to sleep if it's the middle of the night!). If she seems to be having any trouble swallowing the milk, remove the bottle to give her a breather.

This is the basic routine. The parents may have their own particular variations, such as, for instance, using salt to remove all traces of milk from the teat. It might be a good idea to ask them to give you a quick demonstration before you have to look after the baby and make up feeds on your own.

Try to remember that the breastfeeding/bottle-feeding debate has progressed since you had your children. To breastfeed was extremely unfashionable in the 1960s when, in an upwardly mobile society, it was even thought by some that it betrayed working-class roots! And any mother who had the temerity to breastfeed a baby in public was considered a danger to public morals.

Breastfeeding in Public

Whatever your feelings on the subject, try not to feel (or at least, try not to show) embarrassment if your daughter or daughter-in-law chooses to breastfeed her baby in public. This can be difficult for some of us who are not used to the idea – especially perhaps for a grandfather who is not related to the mother by blood. One such confessed to me, rather shamefacedly, that he suddenly realized his disapproval was because of a secret fear that he might find the spectacle arousing.

For those who do find the whole issue a tricky one, I would say ... remind yourself that this is the natural process. It's a wonderful thing that a mother has ready, in no matter what circumstances, a source of nourishment for her baby that is perfect in every way (even the consistency of the milk changing to suit the baby's need throughout the feed). Whilst she is feeding the baby, you can rest assured that she will be totally unaware of anything but the satisfaction of her baby's hunger, and that the last thing she will be thinking of is appearing provocative, either of sexual or shocked reactions.

In the days when breastfeeding in public was not quite the done thing, I remember attending the rehearsal of a chamber-music concert. Between bouts of playing, a young woman cellist sat on a sunny windowsill and freely breastfed her little son, who had been sleeping in a Moses basket by her feet as she played. Her musician companions seemed entirely at ease with the situation – the making of music was all that mattered – and it struck me at the time that the breastfeed-ing seemed as natural as the flow of the music.

When I had my daughter in 1964, my obstetrician said briskly, 'You're planning to go back to work? Then don't even consider breastfeeding.' I have always regretted this decision being taken for me when I was not in any state to consider the alternative. The same obstetrician came in one day and was extremely unpleasant to me, making me burst into tears. 'That's better,' he said. 'You were being too cheerful. I always like my new mothers

to have a good cry. It saves them from having the "baby blues".'
Thank goodness attitudes have radically changed since then!

Peggy Writes

Mum very kindly stayed with me for a while after Sky was
born, and was wonderful – prepared to do anything and
totally willing to fit in with my desire to breastfeed (practically all day at the outset) and have the baby in the bed. She
did far more than her fair share and made sure that everything
was running smoothly, but I have to admit that I was a nightmare. Emotionally, I felt all over the place, and it was she
who took the brunt of my mood swings. I think I'm so sure
of her devotion, that I sometimes take her for granted anyway, and – as all I was thinking about was my new baby –
probably didn't even offer her so much as a cup of tea the
whole time she was staying with us. Typically, she didn't
complain and made the very best of things, but I wish I had
thought about her needs more. Sometimes we parents forget
that grandparents have feelings too!

From the couples I have talked to, I am left in no doubt at all that
tactful help and support during the immediate postnatal period is
one of the most important services grandparents can render. It is
also a wonderful opportunity to get to know the new member of
the family. There's nothing like walking up and down rocking a
baby and having the satisfaction of seeing it fall gently to sleep to
bring out all one's most tender feelings.

Marge: 'When my daughter brought the baby home, I spent the first night with her. There was an utterly terrifying midwife who insisted on covering everything with newspaper. We were both scared stiff of her and really glad when she left for good.'

Sophie: 'After the birth I came into my own. I stayed with the parents for 10 days and did everything. When I left my daughter told me she couldn't have done without me. They bought me perfume and I felt really wanted and valued. My own mother-in-law had been a nightmare. She came to stay after my first baby was born and just sat around chain-smoking and saying, "What are we having for lunch?"'

Kay: 'I stayed with my daughter for the immediate postnatal period. It all came back to me no trouble. I had been like a single parent to my two because my husband buzzed off to Turkey and left me when they were really young. I found I was not as anxious as I had been with mine. I'm so much wiser now than I was then – I was terrible with my own children.'

Martin: 'The other grandparents were the ones who lived near so they got to do all the helping when our granddaughter was born. We visited the hospital just after the birth and thought Tracy was the most gorgeous baby, all six pounds of her, that we had ever seen. But then we had to go back to Virginia. We felt jealous of the other pair, I can tell you. We needn't have, but we did. We would love to have done the babysitting. The only one good thing about the distance

> **between us was that our visits were always treated as a great event and Tracy never took us for granted.'**

Paul Writes

I was 16 when my brother was born and very often I was the only person who could get him to sleep. I would walk up and down with him snuggled into my shoulder and find myself repeating the chant my father had soothed us with when we were young. He was Scottish and he used to murmur, 'Shoo-shuggy, shoo-shuggy, shoo-shuggy ...' When Peggy brought Sky home from the hospital, my putting-babies-to-sleep skills were again in demand. I was actually feeling quite stressed at the time because I had an important first night approaching. As I rocked this new baby in my arms and repeated my father's mantra of 'Shoo-shuggy', I felt myself relax. When my grandson's eyelashes began to droop and his breathing steadied into a quiet rhythm, I found myself as calm as he was. It is very satisfying to help a baby go to sleep.

Help! He Won't Stop Crying
– a Grandparents' Checklist

Pick him up, cuddle him and gently rock him over your shoulder as you walk about the room. Talk gently to him or sing to him to soothe him. Still crying? Could it be that he is:

- hungry?
- tired?
- wet or dirty?
- too hot or cold?
- uncomfortable – might, for instance, the nappy tabs be chafing his legs?
- missing Mummy or Daddy?
- bored?
- in pain?
- ill?

Once you have offered food, changed the nappy, removed or added a layer of clothing, offered stimulation, the chance to sleep or whatever else you think the baby needs, the crying should stop. But if it doesn't, *don't panic* – it's very unlikely to be anything serious. Try playing the baby some music, strapping on the sling (if your back will take it) and walking about, or even – a famous last resort – taking him for a drive in his car seat. After about half an hour of crying, though, it's usually best to contact the parents – if you can. They may have the answer or may at least come to relieve you! But if they are not available and you are concerned that the child might be ill, don't hesitate to call the baby's or your own doctor.

Close Encounters (with Nappies)

The first time you change the nappy of this tiny new baby, you may feel a little nervous because the chances are that you won't have encountered disposables before. Although fabric nappies are being used again to an extent, most parents still prefer disposables.

You may also have the eagle-eyed young parents watching your every move to see that you do it right. Try to take any helpful advice with equanimity. 'No, Dad, not like that! You're putting it on back to front' – 'Mother! Watch out! He's peeing all over you!' Such remarks are just part and parcel of the re-learning experience.

Tricks of the Nappy-changing Trade

To put the changing mat on the floor is probably best because then there is no risk of the baby falling, though you may prefer to use a changing table (in which case, don't turn your back for a second – even with a new, supposedly helpless baby).

You will need:

- a clean nappy
- a nappy-sack to receive the soiled nappy
- a bowl of warm (but not hot) water
- cream
- cotton wool
- tissues or kitchen-roll
- a toy for the baby to look at or hold

What to Do:

1 Get the above ready and in easy reach before you begin.
2 Lie the baby on the mat, talk gently or sing and give it a toy to look at or hold.
3 Undo the tabs of the soiled nappy, one at a time, being careful still to hold the front of the nappy over the baby's genital area (babies will often pee at this moment – and boys can get you in the eye).
4 Now fold the front of the nappy under the baby's bottom, covering up the wet or soiled area. Alternatively, you may want to remove the nappy entirely and put a piece of clean kitchen roll under the baby's bottom.
5 Moisten the cotton wool and wipe gently all over the tummy area and leg creases. Use clean pieces as necessary. With a boy, now wipe over and under the penis and scrotum. With a girl, always wipe from front to back, using a fresh piece of cotton wool if you have to wipe the front again. There is no need to part the labial folds – just wipe carefully over them. (Don't worry, it will all come back to you, unless of course you didn't do it first time around, grandpas!)
6 Now gently hold both of the baby's ankles in one hand and lift the baby's legs up so as to raise the bottom slightly off the mat. Wipe the bottom area until the baby is clean (don't worry if this takes many wipes – just dump the dirty cotton wool in the nappy sack).
7 Put the soiled nappy into the nappy-sack and tie it up.
8 Pat the whole nappy area dry with a clean piece of kitchen roll.

9 Wipe or wash your hands.

10 Working from front to back, smooth cream over the genitals and any particularly sore areas.

11 Slide the back of the clean nappy under the baby with the top at waist height. Most nappies now have a clear indication of back and front on them, but if they don't, remember that the bit with the tabs goes at the back.

12 Holding the front of the nappy in position at one side of the baby's tummy, unfold the tape from the back and stick it over the front of the nappy. Repeat the process on the other side. Check that the nappy is not too tight and the tabs aren't sticking up or down into the baby's flesh when the legs are bent up. There should be room to get one finger between the nappy and the tummy. If the top of the waistband seems to rub, turn it down. (With a boy, it's always wise to make sure that his penis is pointing downwards before securing the nappy, other-wise he may pee over the top of it!)

13 Dispose of the nappy sack in the bin, wash your hands thoroughly and feel very pleased with yourself. YOU'VE DONE IT!

Many parents complain that grandparents will happily hold the baby, gurgle and cluck at it and be the perfect carers until they sense that the nappy needs changing – then they hand it over quick. Remember, parents have to change nappies constantly, day in day out, so they really appreciate it if someone else takes a turn.

Chapter 4

Here We
Go Again

Baby Takes Over

Now you can see the parents trying to establish routines and watch whilst the baby just as routinely breaks them. Again, this is very much the time to offer practical help, but to try to interfere as little as possible. If we are honest with ourselves, how much can we actually remember about parenting? All I can remember is that everything was totally different then in almost every way, except that, like them, we were young, well-meaning people trying to do something perfectly that can only be learned by trial and error.

Each baby is a unique individual who establishes his or her own routine (if such it can be called) in spite of the best efforts of those 'in charge'. Some feed long and lustily and then sleep for civilized periods, while others want to be fed little and often. Some have dreadful colic and others not even a twinge. Some love being bathed and others object vociferously. Some cry endlessly and others lie cooing and gurgling just as in storybooks.

From the 1940s until the late 1960s, Dr Spock's ideas set the childcare agenda. And although the rigidity of his advice has been rather exaggerated by selected quotations taken out of context, there is no doubt that he came down on the side of moderate strictness, which he thought appropriate even with a young baby. According to him, 'confident' parents 'Don't let a sleepy but obstinate baby refuse to be put to bed, because they know very well (mostly from their own childhood) that bedtime is bedtime and that theories of flexibility have very little to do with the situation.'

According to Spock, the baby had to learn to fit into adult life. It had to sleep at certain times and feed at certain times in order to be taught 'who was boss'. Needless to say, like any other system of babycare, this one didn't work perfectly and caused endless anxiety to mothers whose babies refused to behave according to plan. Not to mention the distress of the poor babies left for hours howling in cots and prams.

> Jane: 'I remember the agony of having to listen to my daughter crying in her cot in another room when every instinct in my body made me yearn to run to her. But I was a real brainwashed product of the 1950s and what the man of the house said went. My husband was fiercely jealous of the baby, so naturally he believed in the "let them cry" theory. He told me once, as he left for work, that when he came home he "did not want to see any evidence of a baby in the house". No drying nappies, no toys left lying around and certainly no baby still up – crying or not crying. I can't believe now, being a more liberated woman – even a feminist – that I did as I was told and I ran around the house

in a demented fashion, trying to "remove the evidence". It's not surprising that I left him when my child was two. At last the worm turned!'

Luckily for all, we now live in a much more child-centred society. OK, I hear some of you say, 'But it's gone too far the other way.' Well, maybe – but surely in the long run it's better for the child if we err on the side of being too loving rather than too strict. If your daughter nearly falls over the furniture rushing to lift her baby up at the first squeak, that is her decision. There is nothing worse for parents than a grandparent making remarks that make them feel inadequate. (There is quite enough to make them feel like that without any help from us.) 'My parents make me feel I'm so lax and over-indulgent as a mother. They're always implying that we spoil him' is a cry I've heard from many. A golden rule for us as grandparents is to remember that *they* are the parents and entitled to bring up their children according to their own instincts and principles. *There is no perfect way.*

Everyone tends to believe that they could do it better, and every generation of grandparents seems to think 'there's no discipline nowadays'. You can read this in literature going back thousands of years. But if it really were true, we'd all be savages by now. Don't get me wrong, my husband and I are no saints, and we've found ourselves saying exactly this sometimes, but then we try to be strict with ourselves and rap ourselves over the knuckles for being old fuddy-duddies.

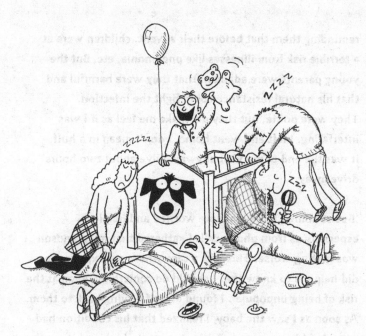

If you have to have a moan, moan to another of your own generation (who might agree with you) rather than to the parents themselves. Only if you observe some practice or omission that could endanger the health or safety of the child should you say something. Then it is your duty to do so and even to act if you think you must.

> 'When my grandson was about a year old, he developed a
> severe chest infection. My daughter and her husband were
> very against antibiotics because they had read of the
> dangers of their overuse. I was visiting them at the time and
> I felt dreadfully worried about his condition. I gently
> suggested that perhaps this was a case for antibiotics,

reminding them that before their advent, children were at a terrible risk from illnesses like pneumonia, etc. But the young parents were adamant that they were harmful and that his natural resistance could fight the infection. They were polite, but they did make me feel as if I was interfering. I left and went home. I don't mean in a huff, it was the end of my visit anyway. I live about two hours' drive away.

'But at home I felt even more worried and helpless, especially as from phone calls I gathered that my grandson was getting worse. This was a case where my experience did help me to know that I should do something, even at the risk of being unpopular. I found myself driving back to them. As soon as I saw the baby, I realized that his condition had considerably worsened. Again, I suggested taking him to the hospital; again I was rebuffed. I was desperate. I walked down to the local chemist, whom I knew well and whose judgement I respected. He asked me if my grandson seemed very absent and dreamy – "Not with you" is how he put it. I said yes. "In that case, I think you should get him seen right away." I walked home determined to do something. Emphatic words with my son-in-law ended with me saying, "Well, remember, if anything happens to that boy, it's your fault." Next thing I knew, they were leaving the house with the baby wrapped in a blanket. "We're taking him to hospital," he said. What seemed like hours passed, and then he phoned me: "You were right; he's got pneumonia. He's on oxygen and they've given him injections of antibiotics. You can come to the hospital if you like."

'When I got to the hospital my daughter and son-in-law
were sitting either side of the bed looking dreadfully shaken.
My grandson was asleep and, although he had an oxygen
mask and a needle device in his foot, the improvement in his
condition was obvious. I felt relief flooding through me and,
although I would have preferred not to be right on this
occasion, I thanked every star in the heavens that experience teaches you some things and that I had risked being
thought an interfering old cow.'

I read recently a young woman's harrowing story of how she and
her sister were left to care for a desperately ill and confused
mother, and just how terrifying that was. She made it clear in the
article that if it hadn't been for her grandparents stepping in and
looking after them, their childhood would have been a complete
disaster.

So there are *sometimes* scenarios that require our constructive
interference. Happily, such extreme cases are comparatively rare
and usually our main role is to support the parents and have fun
with our grandchildren, while providing back-up care. Usually,
despite our busy lives, we still have more time to enjoy the children than when we were parents ourselves. Happily for us, we
can now experience most of the joys of parenting without the
burdens of responsibility.

Peggy Writes

Talking things through with Mum and Paul is always very helpful as they tend to offer constructive ideas and to suggest different approaches based on their own experiences. Often I'm a bit resistant to what they have to say, but that doesn't make our discussions any the less useful. Sometimes I just won't have asked myself enough questions about what I'm doing, or simply haven't been able to think of any alternatives. Talking to them always clarifies my thoughts.

He's So Tiny!

Newborn babies usually sleep for much of the day, even if they don't at night! This can be a bit frustrating for grandparents who arrive bright-eyed and bushy-tailed, wanting to look at and play with their new grandchild. You find yourself gazing at the sleeping infant and willing it to waken, while the poor parent is doing just the opposite. I have even heard tales of mothers catching a grandparent surreptitiously waking the baby! But you would never do that, would you?

Please don't worry if your new grandchild looks rather peculiar at first. Few newborn babies look particularly pretty. Remember that a baby's appearance changes and improves tremendously over the first few weeks. He or she may have somewhat unattractive newborn traits, such as a long (moulded) head, a hairy body and dry, cracked skin, but there is no need to despair – these 'problems' will disappear in a matter of days.

Handling

Be aware of the new baby's wobbly neck. It may sound obvious, and you may think, 'Well, of *course* I'll remember to support her neck,' but at the beginning I had to be reminded at times and I often then had to remind other people, tactfully of course, to do the same.

Tried and tested methods of holding a baby include positioning her in the crook of your arm, with your hand under her bottom and her head resting comfortably on your upper arm. Alternatively, you can place her against your upper chest with her head resting against your breastbone, with one arm supporting her bottom and the other her upper back and neck.

If you want to hold her on your knee to look into her face and talk to her, remember to place one hand gently but firmly at the back of her neck with her spine resting on your forearm. Sometimes very young babies are apt to 'posset' – bring back some milk after a feed. If you know that your grandchild is a 'possety' baby, then it is wise to spread a muslin square over your shoulder (and it is *always* advisable to wear clothes you don't care about when looking after babies).

Colic, a mixture of indigestion and wind, is a condition some new babies suffer from and for which, unfortunately, there is no cure. When a baby has colic it is very hard on both infant and adult as the screams of pain can continue for hours. Sometimes if a breast-feeding mother cuts down on citrus fruits this seems to improve matters, and it is definitely wise for her to steer clear of anything highly spiced.

Here is an old wives' remedy that I found occasionally seemed to help a bit. Lie the baby on his tummy on your lap and gently massage around the waist area. Sometimes you can be rewarded by the blissful sound of breaking wind and the cries stop, though unfortunately not always.

Luckily, colic seems to stop by itself after about three months – occasionally four – but those three months can seem to last a lifetime to the demented parents. So, if your grandchild is a colicky baby, try to give the parents a break as often as you possibly can, because they will certainly need it. It will be distressing for you to listen to the screams, but at least you'll know that for you it's only temporary. Gripe water may seem to help, or dimethicone (a mild anti-acid), but whether these actually relieve the condition or simply satisfy the parents' desire to 'do something' no one really knows.

In our day gripe water contained alcohol! In fact, there is a long and distressing history of doping babies with all sorts of opiates and alcoholic drinks – rag-wrapped corks dipped in laudanum, etc. My own mother used to put a teaspoonful of whisky into our feeding bottles if we cried beyond her capacities of endurance. Although, thankfully, this is not common practice nowadays, I have heard mothers confess to giving their babies a dose of infant paracetamol when perhaps it was not strictly necessary. Better than throwing them out of the window, I admit, but not really a good idea.

Contact

It is quite amazing how much contact you can have with even a very young baby. For instance, she will grasp your fingers immediately. This is purely a reflex action, but nonetheless a thrill, and soon after three months old she will be able to reach out and take hold of an object. Opinions vary about how early babies smile, and often it can be dismissed as wind, but I swear that both my grandchildren smiled at me much earlier than the statutory six weeks!

Remember that a new baby can't focus much beyond nine inches, but by the time she is six months old her sight will be almost as good as an adult's. Amazing isn't it! I do wish someone had explained to me about this lack of focus, because when my daughter was very new her eyes kept rolling about and I was afraid that perhaps she was not quite right in the head.

Looking into a new baby's eyes and making faces and sounds is very good for the infant's development. You may notice little responses – although to you they will be big events, not little at all. You put out your tongue and wiggle it about ... soon she will attempt to put out her tongue. You open your mouth wide and shut it again ... and just watch her try to do the same. Babies learn by imitation, so the more you give them to imitate, the better.

Now is the time to practise your singing skills and to revive all the old, soothing songs that are lurking in your subconscious. Babies *adore* being sung to or chanted at, though at a gentle volume of course!

Hush a-Bye Baby

Some mothers find that putting the baby near to a Hoover or a washing machine soothes it off to sleep. Experts say that this is because the baby was used to all sorts of quite loud noises going on in the womb.

I've noticed that whether to be quiet or not while the baby is sleeping is an issue about which not only grandparents and parents often disagree, but the two parents themselves as well. Some think that the baby must get used to household noises in order to be able to sleep through anything that is going on. Others insist that, unless it is pretty quiet, their babies can't sleep or won't sleep properly. I suspect that, as with other questions, this very much depends on the individual baby. I have known babies who've slept through thunderstorms of startling volume, and others who woke if a fly buzzed in the room.

Also, just like us, babies go in and out of different states of sleep, usually sleeping very heavily for about 15 minutes after they've dozed off, then in cycles of light and heavy sleep thereafter.

Paul Writes

I must own that when Sky was a young baby and I was living with the parents (because I was working in London), at times I thought it a bit over-the-top to run to him when he was only making little snuffly noises and hadn't yet started to cry. I was pretty sure that sometimes he would just have gone back to sleep again by himself, had he been left in peace. Also, I wondered if having utter silence in the house when Sky was sleeping was such a good idea. I understood completely that he needed the quiet to get off properly, but I wondered sometimes if babies who have a completely silent environment are more apt to waken at the slightest sound. As soon as he was asleep we all had to whisper. I suppose I was remembering my own childhood, when no special effort was made to keep things quiet, the house was fairly noisy and chaotic, and my three younger brothers and sisters slept through anything and everything. But maybe that was just the way they were. And anyway, who am I to criticize? I've never had sole responsibility for a young baby. I realize now what a difficult job it is to raise children and how impossible it is to get it just right. My admiration for Sky and Biba's upbringing far outweighs any temptation to carp.

But do be aware of baby's sleeping times if you can, and try not to phone or arrive at inopportune moments. Although it may be difficult for you, it is often best to leave much of the phoning to the parents, or to ring at times that are known to be convenient. It's impossible to avoid doing the wrong thing occasionally, but we should try to be considerate, especially in the early days when the couple are likely to be suffering badly from sleep deprivation themselves. I can remember the rage I felt when, late at night, having at last lulled a baby off to sleep and about to tumble into bed myself, the phone rang and a drunken voice said, 'Hi, just thought I'd ring you for a chat.'

Babies' sleeping habits and routines are often a source of misunderstanding between grandparents and young parents because attitudes in this area have changed so radically in one generation. We were constantly warned that, whatever we did, we MUST NOT TAKE THE BABY INTO BED WITH US! Dreadful dangers were hinted at, such as 'overlaying' that led to their being smothered. We were not to 'pander' to them when they cried, even by staying in the same room as them. And of course, because they were usually not breastfed, a whole routine of bottle-preparation and heating was a nightly task.

My belief is that those of us who are convinced that it was better in our day – 'the baby knew who was boss' – have just blanked out all the sleepless nights they had for various reasons (in the same way that pain is forgotten). There are so many arguments, even among child psychologists, about this subject, that I've come to the conclusion that, as with baby's eating habits, there is no definitive solution to sleeping problems.

Again, so much depends on the individual child's temperament and need for sleep. Also, you cannot expect a child who still has a midday nap to go to sleep at seven o'clock every night. Then there is the factor of illness, which can disrupt sleep patterns for quite a long time. So the whole thing has to be played by ear until a child is three or four, by which time they have usually settled – more or less – into a routine.

But I can still remember when I was a child, the ghastly nights of summer when I lay in bed and saw the daylight springing around the curtains and felt no sleepiness whatsoever. And the dark winter nights, when my door was always firmly shut and the light put out, when I suffered agonies of fear and distress. I am quite sure many of my contemporaries, who were brought up by the same rules, will have experienced similar traumas.

Hannah: 'Right from the beginning with my three I adopted my mother's technique of bedtime rules. It worked well with my brothers and me so, I thought, why not? I firmly believe that parents need time to themselves and I am fed up going to friends' dinner parties that are ruined by stroppy three-year-olds, and where you can't have an uninterrupted conversation. I breastfed all three until they were six months, but from the start I put them in another room to sleep. OK, it meant leaping up and down a bit for a while, and I don't pretend I wasn't pretty exhausted, but after they were weaned, they soon realized that once they were in bed, unless they were ill, that was it. Now that they are five, four, and two, they are into the bath at seven, in bed by half-past, and they know that I am incommunicado till the morning. If they wake before we do, they just look at books until I come to them. It works very well.'

Josie: 'We took our first into bed with us straight away. Oh, she had a Moses basket, a cot and everything, but I was breastfeeding her and I just felt I wouldn't know what she needed unless she was right beside us. I found that I got so that I hardly wakened when she fed. It was lovely and cozy and such a nice feeling to have a sleepy, relaxed baby in bed with us. She hardly ever cried, I think as a direct result of being so near me. Not only that, but I've read that it's the natural thing to do and there is much less likelihood of cot death when the baby is near you all the time.'

So, it appears that even among mothers themselves it's horses for courses.

Chapter 5

The Techno Babe

Gizmos, Gadgets and What Not To Do with Them

For first-time grandparents it's a bewildering scene technologically. All kinds of baby equipment are now on the market that didn't exist when we were young. Some of it is over-priced and gimmicky, but many items are brilliantly designed for the safety of the child. So do allow the new parents to instruct you fully in their safety routines and to coach you on how everything works. And if you don't understand something, just keep asking until you do.

My daughter and son-in-law's baby monitor looks like a miniature pub fruit machine – all knobs and coloured lights flashing on and off in a semi-circle. Unfortunately, at first, I had a dreadful habit of turning it to 'Mute' – by mistake, I promise you!

I have just read in *The Guardian* an article about Jodie Foster investing £300,000 in a high-tech baby monitor that will allow her to see and talk to her baby son, and be seen and talked to by him, no matter where in the world she is on location – long-distance mothering, as it were.

As a cheaper alternative, one famous firm offers a sound and vision monitor for a few hundred pounds, which allows you not only to hear but also to see your child from any part of the house – and even from the garden. The writer of *The Guardian* article declares that she has never been one to go in for monitors, because if there is anything really wrong her son yells loud enough for her to hear him anyway. She also says that research suggests that all this hi-tech equipment is part of a modern tendency to over-protect our children, making them grow up 'timid and dependent' – actually 'mollycoddled' is the word she uses (she sounds a bit like a grandmother already!). But she makes a valid point when she says that gadgets and gizmos are good if they make parents and children happier and safer, but are a dangerous extravagance if they become a replacement for ordinary human contact.

Of course most couldn't afford such extravagances, even if they wanted to. One set of parents I know has a particularly curious toddler. They are quite hard up and, at some expense, had all their cupboards and the fridge fitted with baby-proof catches. To their exasperation, the grandparents couldn't or wouldn't understand their instructions as to how to undo these gently, but just wrenched and broke them all. The only person who was pleased about that was the toddler!

Safety covers for electric power points are often treated with similar contempt, as if the parents are being over-fussy: 'I just used to smack your hand if you went anywhere near the plugs. You could do the same' is the kind of remark grandparents too often make.

Strap Up Your Troubles

Do take full instruction in the fastenings and strapping of buggies, car seats, highchairs, etc. My granddaughter's car seat has a particularly tortuous system whereby you have to align two metal parts before slotting them into the clip in front of her tummy. And you can be sure that, just at the crucial moment when you have carefully aligned them, she will wriggle, and you're back to square one. Any manufacturer of car seats, buggies, etc. who could come up with grandparent-friendly fastenings would make a fortune. I don't just mean making them simpler to understand, but easier on our backs, as currently we have to bend and twist to fasten them properly. I can't help feeling that there must be some way of making them simpler to fasten, while still keeping up safety standards.

To her alarm, my daughter used to find that, although I had fastened my grandson into his car seat all right, I had omitted to secure the seat itself, which was potentially lethal. Naturally, I was horrified when I realized what I'd done – or rather, had not done.

In fact, parents often complain that grandparents fail to learn the ins and outs of modern gadgets.

'My parents' inefficiency with baby equipment just follows the pattern of their ineptitude with anything technical. They have an answerphone they forget to switch on, a mobile that never leaves the house, a VCR they don't know how to record with, a fax machine but never a spare fax roll (and even if they did have one, they wouldn't know how to insert it), and an expensive multimedia computer that they use like a typewriter. When I nag them to use the baby's equipment properly, they just make remarks like, "Oh, don't bother us with all these 'techno' things. You slept in a drawer in another room and I didn't have a baby monitor for you" or "Yes, yes, I *understand*! I'm not stupid. I'll make sure everything is plugged in – just go away!" or "There *were* no car seat belts when you were a baby, and *you* survived." It's hopeless. If it weren't so important, it would be funny, but it's not when it's a matter of your child's safety.'

On a less serious note, one grandmother reports her dilemma with a folding buggy:

'I was taking my grandson for an outing to the local town. My daughter put his folded-up buggy in the boot, having taken great care first to show me how to unfold it. I carefully fastened him into his car seat – and got that right (having tortured my back fastening all the straps) – and we set off.

'In town, all goes well. I unfold the pushchair and manage to strap him in correctly. There is a slight moment of uncertainty while I work out how to release the wheel-brake, but it turns out to be quite easy. I push him by the river, let him out to feed the ducks, take him to the toyshop, and allow him to toddle round and have a look at everything before he chooses something. (I have permission from his parents to buy him a toy, by the way.) Then we go to a café for a drink, where he behaves beautifully, and I enjoy the admiring looks and remarks he attracts. Back at the car, I take him out of his pushchair and fasten him safely into his car seat again, remembering to do up the straps correctly. I feel quite proud and efficient. It has begun to rain, so I shut the car door saying, 'Nanny will just be a moment,' and turn to put the pushchair away in the boot. That's when the trouble starts. I had only seen my daughter *unfold* the darn thing and had wrongly presumed that, if you did the opposite, it would fold up again. But no, nothing so simple. I push it, I pull it, I waggle every available knob and lever. The rain grows ever heavier. My grandson begins to look rather anxious inside the car. Smoothing my face into an untroubled smile, I open the door and give him his new toy to play with – happy boy. Back to the uncollapsible pushchair. Sweating, I try to force it to fold up, but it stubbornly remains whole. 'Right!' I think, teeth gritted in John Cleeseian fashion, 'I'll put the bloody thing in the car just as it is.' I open the back. It will go in only if I leave the boot open, and that wouldn't be safe or a great idea in the now torrential rain. Damn! OK. Don't panic. You're only stuck in a car park with no one in sight. It's lashing rain and the novelty of the toy won't last for ever, quite apart from the fact that your daughter will begin to panic if you don't get back soon. Glancing wildly around, I see, like a mirage in the distance, a young couple passing the entrance to the car park and – what is this? They are pushing a toddler in a buggy that looks very like the one that's giving me all this grief. Wildly, I wave at them. They look at me suspiciously. I shout and raise my arms in a praying gesture. They hurry their steps slightly to get away from this local loony. Casting pride to the wind, I run up to them and explain what has happened. Can they help? They can, thank goodness, and as a slight salve to my *amour propre* the father has quite a struggle with the buggy before he manages to fold it up. "It's very different from ours. With ours, you just kick the lever at the side." I only told my daughter about this episode quite a few months later, when I must say she had the good grace to laugh.'

Peggy Writes

Both my mother and I are a bit absent-minded, so I often remind her to do up straps, etc. Not that I really think she'll forget – she makes a point of overriding her absent-mindedness where the children are concerned – but because I think that, sure as fate, the one time I don't remind her will be the one time that I need to. Superstition really, and a sense that I am not taking ultimate responsibility if I don't. In fact, when my children have tumbled out of the buggy (twice, to my shame), it was because I had forgotten to strap them in.

There are many smaller items of equipment that you can only properly find out about when you stay with the family for a few days, so it pays to watch carefully when the parents are using them themselves. They will usually have found out any shortcuts that can be made and are careful to avoid those that cannot. If the baby is bottle-fed, find out about their sterilizing equipment, and about the scalding of beakers, cups, etc. for older babies – if that is what they do. Oh, and by the way, be sure also to find out how beaker tops seal. If you don't, you can prepare yourself for smelly or sticky leakages in your bags and pockets. Needing a clean nappy and finding it is soaked in orange juice is not a happy experience. You will also undergo the delight of discovering whether you are strong enough to snap down the spouts on 'travel-safe' plastic beakers. I can unsnap them but have great difficulty in snapping them down again, especially after they have been chewed out of shape.

Dear reader, don't worry if at this point you think I've gone off my head and you don't know what on earth I'm on about. You'll soon learn!

Here is a list of a few things I take on walks with my grand-children:

- Wet wipes in a plastic bag or box
- Lots of tissues
- Two spare nappies (or if toilet-training, then a complete change of clothes – and even a potty!)
- A beaker of water or juice (top snapped down firmly!)
- The same of milk (ditto re top)
- Slices of apple in a plastic box
- Tiny brown bread Marmite sandwiches or another favourite snack
- Stale bread for ducks (which grandchildren usually eat)
- A toy, like a ball
- The favourite toy of the moment
- The mobile phone (my daughter bought me this – can't think why)
- My purse
- The buggy (equipped with rain or sun attachments)
- Oh, and don't forget the grandchild (suitably clad in removable layers)!

All these items and the many more collected en route, go into the net at the back of the buggy, lurk in the folds of the rain hood or hang in bags from the handles. I have even been known to carry an old piece of terry towelling. What for? For wiping raindrops off swings and slides, of course! One word of warning, though. Before letting the child out of the seat, make sure you have removed anything hanging from the handles, otherwise the buggy will inevitably tip-up, crash down on your shins, and you'll end up with the orange juice-soaked nappy scenario.

As for pushchair brakes, *do* remember to put them on at *all* times, even if you only stop for a second. One grandfather learned this through bitter experience:

'It was the first time I had been trusted out alone with both of my grandchildren. Alice was about three and James a year old. We went to feed the ducks. I parked the pushchair at the edge of the pond and with one hand started to fish out the bread from my pocket, still holding my granddaughter with my other. Suddenly, she pulled her hand away and darted off. Of course I turned around to try to grab at her. Behind me I heard a splash and a kind of gurgle. I swear it all happened in a trice. When I turned back all I could see were the wheels of the buggy sticking up out of the water, which, luckily, was very shallow. Still holding on to Alice, I scooped the buggy out with baby attached and, do you know, he was fine – not even crying. I nearly had a heart attack I got such a fright, but it taught me a lesson as I'd forgotten to put the brakes on when we stopped. When I got home I had some explaining to do I can tell you. It was a while before I was trusted again.'

Halfway Up the Stairs

Stair gates are another safety device one has to be careful about because, if you push them past a certain point, the bolt can miss the hole so that the gate remains unsecured. One young mother who is particularly fit tells me that, to save time and trouble, she vaults over her stair gates – unless of course she happens to be carrying a child or a full potty at the time.

When the child gets to the stage of not needing the stair gate any more, it is a good idea to teach her or him to go down the stairs backwards on their tummy. I know it sounds strange, but this crabwise method is safest. Sometimes they prefer to bump down on their bottoms, which is not too dangerous (except if they do it so enthusiastically that they topple over). Supervision is essential until both the child and parents are confident that stairs can be negotiated safely.

Paul Writes

I can spend hours playing on our stairs with my grandchildren – one of a whole series of rituals that have to be observed every time they come to stay. We go up to the half landing and Sky and Biba take turns rolling the top of the laundry basket down the stairs, while I run ahead of it shouting, 'Oh, Oh, Oh!' and they laugh their heads off. But the rule is that they must both sit down before they play this game, otherwise in the heat of the moment they might tumble headlong after me.

Then there is the game where they scramble ahead of me up the stairs, trying to be so quick that I can't tap them on the bottom. They have never yet asked to slide down the banisters, and I wouldn't encourage them to do that. I was holding my little sister on a banister once to help her to slide down and, because she was struggling, she fell over the other side! Luckily for her and for me, the stairs weren't very high and there was a huge pile of washing on the hall floor which cushioned her fall. When, terrified, I peeped over at her she was laughing up at me. I can still remember the relief flooding through me. Especially as this was the same sister whose feet I had been partly responsible for scalding. I was filling the bath for her and, being just a child myself, I didn't know to run the cold tap first. I turned my back for a moment, she came dancing in and – before I realized it – she had leapt into the bath, just as I was about to say, 'Don't get in yet.' Both of her feet blistered terribly and she couldn't walk for ages. To this day, I still feel guilty about it!

Sitting Pretty

High chairs are still more or less as they were in our day but much better in design, some of them coming apart to form a chair and little table for when the baby is older. They are also improved by safety features, like being well-balanced and having straps and harnesses. Yet it is so easy to dump the baby in a high chair and feel that he or she is then entirely safe, forgetting that they must also be strapped in carefully. And don't forget the strap that goes between the legs. At first I kept finding that I had only fastened the waist strap and had then to start all over again.

Anyway, think of the fun you'll have trying to unstrap them when the clippy bit is all covered in gooey baby food. A very good idea is to spread a plastic 'splat mat' beneath the entire high chair area, because you'll usually find most of the baby's meal on it afterwards. One family of my acquaintance had a dachshund that was of fairly average weight before their first child was born. By the time the second was in the high chair, the dog was twice his normal size. He had reached these mammoth proportions simply by lurking underneath the chair and scoffing up all the tit-bits that came his way. Nor was the baby slow to realize that he could drop any food he didn't like – green vegetables, for instance – and that it would disappear as if by magic.

The Learning Curve

If all this advice about safety sounds a bit daunting, don't despair. Remember you don't have to learn it all at once. It is a gradual process and the more time you can spend with your grandchildren (if they want you to, of course!), the easier learning will be. I'm sure an open mind helps enormously. That was something I attained slowly because I have to admit that at first I was inclined to think that some of the equipment was a little over the top. Especially when my daughter and son-in-law – at vast expense – bought an electronic gadget that went under the baby's mattress to monitor his breathing. The idea was that if the breathing stopped, a high-pitched alarm went off. The trouble was that all of us – including the parents, I have to say – would forget to switch

it off before we took the baby out of his Moses basket. 'Wheeee!' the alarm would go and a pale-faced person would rush in from another room to see if the baby was still breathing, only to find a red-faced person holding the baby and saying feebly, 'Sorry, I forgot to switch it off.'

I did notice that when the second grandchild arrived, the breathing monitor seemed no longer in evidence (I later found out that they had given it to the hospital, where they thought it could be put to better use). But it depends – they felt they needed reassurance the first time around, and with so much talk of cot death, it is easy to understand why.

Chapter 6

They're Wonderful Parents, But ...

What Grandparents Really Think

There is a startling uniformity about grandparents' criticisms of parents and vice versa. Finding this out had a salutary effect on me, making me question the prejudices and preconceptions of both generations. Paradoxically – and positively – it seems to be the collective opinion of grandparents that today's parents do it better than they did.

I think the conflicts between parents and grandparents are worth looking into. Hopefully, beginning to understand how differences occur can help us to avoid their reoccurrence in the future.

Let's consider the main 'beefs' of the older generation:

- 'They never say no to them.'
- 'They allow them to interrupt all the time.'
- 'Their house is a mess.'

They let him watch far too much television.

- 'They let them watch too much television.'
- 'They don't put them to bed early enough.'
- 'They let them eat rubbish because they don't cook like we did.'

And now the things they most admire:

- 'They are much closer to their children than we were.'
- 'They listen to them properly. They had to be seen and not heard.'
- 'They've got more time for their children; they don't spend all their time cooking and cleaning.'
- 'They're much more involved with their education than we were.'
- 'Fathers play such an active role now.'

- 'They both work and yet somehow they still manage to be wonderful parents.'

It seems that the very things we criticize parents for are inseparable from the things we most admire. Poor parents, they can't win! But then, in my experiences, mixed feelings are part and parcel of every family relationship.

Some Critical Quotes from Grandparents

'It's a shame they have no garden for the children to play in. And they let them watch too much television, especially cartoons. I'm worried about their eyesight.'

'They don't make sure he has enough exercise. He never walks anywhere.'

'They don't cook enough fresh food – it's all chicken nuggets, fish fingers and oven chips.'

'It's not what they eat I object to, it's *the way* they eat. With their mouths open and just stuffing it all in. And they don't make them sit at table, they just eat any old where.'

'I don't think they discipline her enough – especially over food. They cook about a million different meals for her and bring dish after dish, which she rejects out of hand. She's really pernickety. With my children I gave them one thing and if they didn't eat it up then it was too bad. They didn't get any more. I couldn't afford it for one thing.'

'They're not marvellous in the potty department. My granddaughter is only just clean and dry at three and a half. Mine were all fully toilet trained at 18 months.'

'I sometimes have to fight to get my point over. When my daughter was trying to dry up her milk, I did have one triumph though. I suggested she try Epsom salts. "Oh, Mum!" she said and gave me a derisive look. Then the midwife came and said "Epsom salts, that's what you need." I must say I *preened*. Although the same midwife also said that my daughter should put cabbage leaves on her breasts. That sounded positively medieval to me.'

'They made us feel that they didn't want us to interfere, because they'd read all the books and done all the classes and therefore knew much more than us about childcare. But later we were told off for not coming round more to help them.'

'They are so inconsistent with their discipline. As quickly as I learn their rules for the children, they change the goal posts. They give in too much to tantrums and they make a rod for their own backs. We're afraid that later on the children will think that all they have to do is be very difficult and then they'll get anything they want.'

'They undermine any discipline I that try to instil in them in my own home. They keep saying, "They're only little" – but they have to learn the rules sometime, don't they? After all, they're going to have to do some things they don't want to in later life.'

'They seem to make a mountain out of a molehill of looking after their children. It all seems like such an impossible task. Were we like that? I can't think that we were. But maybe I've forgotten.'

'When I babysit I always take my rubber gloves and find myself scrubbing away and cleaning things out – especially the fridge. It really amuses us that they have all these anti-bacterial sprays that they just spray on top of all the gunge.'

'There are no rules about bedtime. I find it a bit daunting when I go to babysit that they're still up. Mine were all put to bed at seven o'clock.'

'I don't agree with the children sleeping with them.'

'I feel they're not quite strict enough with the toddler about safety. He won't let you hold his hand, and I think that should have been insisted on because he's so nippy and I'm terrified on the road with him. Those reins we had for ours should never have gone out of fashion. They were great.'

'My wife can say things without them taking offence, but if I say anything, all hell breaks loose. I daren't reprove any of my grandchildren if they're naughty without falling out with the parents, so I just have to take myself off for a walk. Somehow criticism from a grandfather seems to hurt more.'

Praise from Grandparents

'I admire the way working parents organize their day.'

'I can't get over how wonderful my son-in-law is with his children and how he shares all the work. He is so careful too about washing his hands carefully before he touches the baby. I remember my first husband took a week off work when my third child was born – a very unusual thing to do in the sixties. I was really surprised and touched, but the first time I asked him to fetch me something he refused indignantly, saying, "Listen, I'm on holiday." '

'I think they are much better about toilet training than we were. I remember making mine sit on the potty till their bottoms were red-ringed. I suppose it was almost essential for sanity (and drying space) to get one child trained before the other arrived needing those terrible terry nappies plus linings, plastic pants and all. Do you remember trying to get poo out of the elasticized, puckered legs of plastic pants?'

'I think they are great with their discipline. They think about issues and talk things through with them. They don't shout and they don't smack – well, hardly ever!'

'I think they are brilliant parents and much better than I was. I was always trying to keep up standards and worrying about the future, but they are much more relaxed. They have more fun with their children and they live for the moment with them.'

'They are not over-protective, like I was. Oh, they worry more about letting them out on their own, and no wonder with all the horror stories you hear, but they're not forever warning them about falling down and hurting themselves like I did. I made them all rather timid, I think.'

'They are very clever at preventing sibling rivalry. We weren't quite as bad as our own parents – because I remember my sister telling me she was traumatized for life when she heard my mother, who was pregnant with me, say, "Thank God that brat will be in school by the time this one arrives." But even our generation didn't consider the older child's feelings properly. My son and his wife did all sorts of clever things to make the older one feel important and included.'

'Yes, I think they're better than we were. We were too hide-bound. Mind you, more laid-back parenting did begin to happen in the sixties. And so did disposable nappies – of a kind. They were huge and clumsy, though. When I suggested them, my husband said, "No son of mine is going to wear paper on his bottom." '

'They have a much more relaxed style than we had. I think I was always nagging my three, saying, "Get to bed! Now!" and things like that.'

'I think they've struck a perfect balance with her upbringing. She is really well mannered. And they have taught her very well because she's not shy either.'

'She doesn't worry and fuss as I did.'

'My daughter's partner is a really great cook – does it all, and the children love it.'

'Just after the baby was born, I was really impressed with my son-in-law and how he coped. Our daughter was very ill for a while and he did everything. The much greater involvement of the father is the best thing about parenting nowadays, and I'm sure it starts with the father being present at the birth. I had to pay to be allowed to be present at the birth of my third child! Before that I just wasn't allowed near. The thinking among obstetricians at the time was that if we saw what we had done to our wives, we would become impotent!'

The cheering news for new mothers and fathers is that, taken as a whole, grandparents' praise for their parenting seems to outweigh any criticisms. Although my husband and I have our moments of carping, our personal feeling is certainly one of deep admiration for my daughter and son-in-law. Yes, I know you may be think-ing, 'Well you have to say that,' but when we see how committed and caring they are with their children, it makes us feel that they are professional where we were amateur.

I can remember doing really unorthodox things like putting my daughter to sleep in the dressing rooms of theatres, then waking her to go home after the show. I smoked until she was about 12, and used to get really impatient with her when she flapped her

They're so much closer to their children these days.

hands about and complained that she was choking. I drove her all over the country with me and we stayed in some pretty terrible theatrical 'digs' together. And I was very strict about her being quiet in the flat because of neighbours – I used to make her take off her shoes at the front door. Because her father and I split up when she was two, and I didn't meet Paul till she was 13, I was more or less a single parent and couldn't have managed nearly as well if it hadn't been for the support of a grandparent.

When my father retired from general practice in Glasgow, all I had to do was call him in an emergency and he would drive hundreds of miles to be with us. He was my daughter's male role model and she couldn't have had a better one. They loved each other with an all-consuming passion, and so if I had to work away for a while I knew that she was completely happy and secure with her beloved 'Grampa'. Later, we managed to get him a small flat right across the road from us, where he lived for several happy years and helped Peggy (and me!) through her teenage years.

Peggy Writes

It can be difficult for parents and grandparents always to get on because both care so deeply about the children's welfare and therefore feel it is their duty not to be mutely polite, but to express whatever they believe is in the children's best interests. Children are not a casual subject – politics and religion pale into insignificance as bones of contention – and when decisions are critical and irreversible, for instance to immunize or not to immunize, the mildest people can become irritable. This is only to be expected. I don't know of any parents who haven't disagreed with their own parents over something or other. It's part and parcel of everybody adapting to a new situation, and probably quite a healthy process.

Paul Writes

Although I have to admit to making some small criticisms, I really feel I have very little right to. Overall, I have tremendous admiration for the parenting of my stepdaughter and her husband. I am in the strange position of having three daughters: a stepdaughter, an adopted daughter, and a blood daughter – none of whom I have brought up myself for their complete childhoods. I have terrible guilt feelings about this and I cannot entirely blame the vicissitudes of a theatrical career and two marriages for my omissions. It is only since I have become a step-grandparent and been an integral part of my grandchildren's lives from birth, that I realize what a hopeless parent I was when I was young and self-obsessed. My adopted daughter (from my first marriage) said to me the other day, 'What age were you when you married my Mum? Twenty-three? Well, no wonder!' I am trying hard to make up for this lack of proper parenting to all of my children. Although they are now grown up, I hope it might not be too late to become the father to them that I always should have been. Being a grandfather has brought it all home to me.

Paul is not alone in feeling that being a grandparent gives one a second chance to 'get it right'. I know I do, and many I've spoken to say that they feel it gives them an opportunity to rectify past mistakes or omissions. Several young mums and dads have expressed surprise at their parents' change of attitude when they move into the third generation: 'She had so little patience with us when we were little, but she'll play for hours with my kids.' 'He's a much better grandad than he was a dad.' 'We were quite scared of my dad – he was so short-tempered – but his grandchildren can get away with murder,' are not untypical remarks.

In life, you get so few second chances to do things better, but being a grandparent is one of them. As George Eliot wrote, 'It is never too late to be what you might have been.'

Chapter 7

They're Wonderful Grandparents, But ...

What Parents Really Think

Much of the interest and the fun of working on this book has been in hearing both sides of the story – from grandparents and from their children (often told to me in no uncertain fashion). Both my daughter and I were slightly nervous before we started collaborating on it, because we realized that the only way we would succeed in getting other people to open up was to be open with each other about the things that irritate us. Before a single word was written, we had to make a pact that – above all – we would be honest and try not to take offence, no matter what crawled out of the woodwork.

To our great surprise, the process has had all sorts of healthy side-effects and, far from causing problems between us, many seem to have been resolved. One hazard of our always having had such a close relationship (single mum, only child) is that we have often been afraid of hurting each other, so that instead of coming out with something, we were inclined to pussyfoot around each other until we reached boiling point. These crises happened very rarely, but were extremely painful for us both when they did: lots of tears; lots of apologies.

Paul Writes

I could often see that Peggy and her mother were not bringing things out into the open. I could sense my wife wanting to say something but keeping it in and getting more and more tense as a result. Sometimes she would confide to me that she was worried about something Peggy was doing and I'd say, 'Well, have you told her?' and Claire would answer, 'No, I don't want to hurt her feelings. She might take offence.' Then Peggy would tell me the same thing from her point of view. It was as if neither of them could bear the slightest criticism from each other without it being very traumatic. I do think they are both much better now at airing opinions before they become grievances. Perhaps every family should write a book, though it might sometimes run the risk of being a kill rather than a cure!

We've gradually become aware that, if points of view are expressed before they become criticisms – and above all if you can laugh about them with one another – then many problems inherent in the generation gap can be avoided. It has helped us immensely to write this book, and we hope it will be of help to you to read it.

Let's consider some criticisms from parents:

- 'They make us feel guilty.'
- 'They undermine our discipline by being over-indulgent.'
- 'They imply that their discipline was much more effective.'
- 'They over-excite the children.'
- 'They buy the children unsuitable things.'
- 'They are unwilling to learn about modern approaches and equipment.'

They always buy the children unsuitable things.

But thankfully it's not all negative:

- 'They've got such patience with them.'
- 'They show them wonderful things, tell them stories and teach them.'
- 'They are always interested in the things the children do and achieve.'
- 'They give them an extra sense of security.'
- 'They give *us* an extra sense of security.'
- 'They take them off our hands when we need a break.'

Some Critical Quotes from Parents

'My mother-in-law always makes me feel as though I'm not managing, and sometimes my own mother isn't that much better. Between the two of them, I sometimes think I'm the most incompetent mother in the world. They're always saying things like, "Are those clothes you're putting on him aired properly?" and "You need to clean out that loo – it's filthy." Oh, I feel dreadful saying this because they do help me a lot, but just sometimes I wish they could do it without making me feel that I can't cope.'

'Just when we're battling with our two-year-old's tantrums about chocolate and insisting he can't have any, we turn our backs and the next minute we see his Grandad slipping him some and winking at him like they're joined in some kind of a conspiracy against us.'

'They say things like, "You've got to let them know who's boss," and "If you ask me, she needs a good smacking. I used to stand no nonsense with you." They are not willing to open their minds to the fact that there are many kinds of discipline other than physical abuse.'

'I'm very fond of my father-in-law and he's a wonderful grandpa, but he will arrive just after a meal or just before their bedtime, and swing them around his head and play wild chasing games with them. They love it, of course, but then he goes off to the pub or home to his quiet flat and I'm left with three hysterical monsters on my hands.'

'I said to my mother the other day, "Mother, perhaps marbles, penknives and party poppers are not the best gifts – he's only three," and she looked really hurt. Next time she came she didn't bring him anything at all. Now all she buys him are sweets but, sure as fate, she brings those highly coloured ones with lots of E numbers in. And she seems to have no imagination about accidents waiting to happen. I told her I tried not to let him run about with pointed objects – after she'd given him a biro from her bag. Another time, I asked her to hold his hand when he was walking along a quite a high wall. She just laughed and said that I was a fusspot and that I must let him learn to negotiate danger.'

'We always have to check everything after they've done it – like fastening the children's seatbelts, etc. And the wiring in their house is lethal. We've nagged them and nagged them, but they don't seem to pay any attention. It makes us unwilling for the children to go to them unless we're there to supervise, which is a shame because they love nothing better than to visit "Nan and Gampa" in their big, old house. It's so exciting for them. There's a lovely garden, but unfortunately there's also a lovely garden pond – and usually lots of slug pellets, too.'

'They're so strict with them. They want them to sit up at table and be quiet while we all have an adult conversation. Of course it never works out and they end up getting really short-tempered.'

'She says things like, "Well, my daughter doesn't seem to have any problems getting hers to bed. Mind you, she's got her rules and she sticks to them. The children know where they are with her. You're just a big softie, aren't you." She says it laughing, but she means it all right. When she leaves, I punch the sofa cushions.'

'They drink rather a lot and so we're scared to leave the kids in their charge. They're not alkies or anything like that, but they love the odd glass of wine of an evening, or should I say the odd bottle.'

'Whenever they help us out financially, which I must admit is quite often, they always make us feel that we have to be terribly grateful and that we are an enormous drain on their resources. We are terribly grateful, of course, but it gets to be a strain to have to demonstrate it all the time.'

Asthma Care

Unfortunately increasing numbers of children seem to be suffering from asthma, and although this can't easily be prevented, there are a number of things you can do to avoid exacerbating the condition:

- Never smoke around your grandchildren.
- Keep your home reasonably dust-free and vacuum before your grandchild comes.
- Don't buy a furry pet for the child or for yourself if you know that your grandchild is susceptible to asthma or eczema.
- Change your grandchild's bedding regularly and avoid giving him a feather pillow and duvets, or old blankets.

Peggy Writes

Some disagreements stem from everyone wanting to be too perfect. Often parents believe that if they don't have opinions and seem to know exactly what they are doing, then the grandparents will think they can't manage. Grandparents too are keen to show that they are 'up to the job' and therefore strive to involve themselves – sometimes more than is welcome. However, even if everyone doing their best can become a bit tense at times, it is far, far better than the alternative. Better grandparents who 'interfere' than who disappear.

Some Admiring Quotes from Parents

'My mother has been my rock throughout my life, but especially since I became a single parent. She looked after Katie while I worked, gave up her own job to do it, and she has never, ever – even for a moment – made me feel as if it has been anything but a great privilege.'

'I love to hear them talking to the children and showing them things. My Mum teaches them all the funny little rhymes that she used to sing to me – and lots that I've never heard before.'

'We find they can help us to iron out problems that arise. We talk things over with them and very often one or other suggests something that will be of use. When our 14-year-old daughter was going through a very difficult patch, I was moaning to them about her and my father said, "Well, dear, you've got two choices: either you can stay on her side, in which case you will have some influence, or you can go against her, in which case, you won't." It was so clear, so succinct, that advice, that I realized it takes one a good few years to arrive at such wisdom.'

'Whenever one of the children cuts a tooth or does well at something, I'm on the phone to their grandmas. I get nearly as much pleasure out of their reaction as I do from the children's achievements.'

'I was going mad. A single parent, two young children and what do I have to go and do? Fall in love. Yeah – head over heels. It was terrible because I had no time to see him and if he came to the flat I felt so guilty and the girls would get upset. It was an awful situation. Then my Mum suddenly says, "I'll take them off your hands for a week, Cheryl, then you can go and spend some time with your boyfriend. It'll do you good." I was gob-smacked! I didn't even think she knew about him! In the event it didn't work out, but I don't think I'd have realized that so soon if I hadn't had that week.'

'Our two always threaten us that they're going to run away and live with their grandparents. Their house is like their second home. They feel so secure there. Once I heard my mother-in-law telling them a story that she would get a cottage "on Canada Hill, where you can live with me. And there'll be a money tree in the garden." The youngest said, "We don't need a cottage, Granny. We'll just live with you here." '

'My mother-out-of-law, as I call her, because Julia and I aren't married, always says she thinks the ideal grand- mother "should put her hand in her pocket and keep her mouth shut". She lives up to that. The number of times she's helped us out financially and yet she never casts it up. She's great. But I just wish she wouldn't smoke so much. I don't like the smoke around the children.'

'We all adore her. I think our youngest summed it up without knowing it. He was trying to say "Granny Heather", which is the name we all use, but it came out as "Granny Heaven".'

'I was very ill during my second pregnancy. My husband had to work abroad for months and I was in despair. Suddenly there were my parents at the door. They scooped up my three-year-old and me, packed all our stuff, locked up my house and drove me to their house. Mum put me to bed and told me not to worry any more. She and Dad looked after us for weeks and still managed to do their work, which luckily is home-based. They were terrific. It was wonderful to

revert to being a child again myself and to be looked after.
I'll never forget what they did.'

'I went through a terrible, acrimonious divorce. Then
eventually I started living with another man. Throughout all
of this my greatest support, especially as far as the children
were concerned, was my ex-mother-in-law! Although she
loves her son, she could see there were two sides to the
split-up and she helped me and the children through one of
the worst patches of our lives. I couldn't believe that
anyone could be that magnanimous.'

Help or Interference?

So far as our grandparenting is concerned, we must guard against
any resemblance to the girl in the old rhyme: 'When she was
good, she was very, very good and when she was bad, she was
horrid.' Like any other family relationship, it's hard to reach perfect equilibrium. Like parents with their own children, grandparents must continually tread a tightrope between interference and
constructive help.

Our parents' generation tended to be far less inhibited about
interference, and grandparents (especially grandmothers) felt it
was their place to be consulted about everything. One reason for
this may have been the lack of public advice to new parents, so
that the older generation felt it incumbent upon them to teach
from experience.

In the 1930s a book appeared entitled *Letters from a Grandmother*, which purported to reproduce real letters exchanged by a grandmother and her daughter, but which was in fact a parenting manual. Its tone is sugary, and anything approaching reality is shrouded in euphemism. Before the wedding night, the mother writes to her daughter:

> *It's sweet of you to thank me for my 'good advice'. My dear, all along I've tried to give you little glimpses of the beautiful side of mating and the passing on of life ... your father was a good bit older than I was, but in spite of that wasn't I frightened in my first year of married life!*

When her daughter becomes pregnant, the attempt at practical advice is as follows:

> *Don't you worry, Marjory, but keep your mind confident and cheerful. There are lively little babies tumbling into the world every minute, and though it's often a painful business, most of the mothers forget the pain pretty quickly 'for joy that Man is born'. Now, Marjory, you're a sensible girl, and this adventure that is before you is just a natural business.*
>
> Letters of a Grandmother – glimpses into a happy home, Hilda
> M Halliday, MRCS, LRCP, DPH

So much for passing on any hints about labour. But perhaps this reticence is not that surprising, because if we go back a bit further, we find a woman who was married in 1917 saying in an interview,

When I was expecting my first baby, I didn't know
whether it was going to come out of my tummy or where
it was going to come out of. And this is perfectly true and I
was twenty-seven and a half.

A Century of the Scottish People – 1830 to 1950, T C Smout

My own grandmother, although she was a Victorian, was much more candid about things, though, interestingly, she was only open with me, her granddaughter, and not with her own daughter, who was brought up in the usual hush-hush manner as far as sexuality was concerned.

My grandmother told me in some detail about her wedding night and her four births. She remembered particularly how terribly shy and nervous her husband was when he got into bed with her that first night: 'He was literally trembling, so I just put my leg over him.'

She was equally outspoken to any young man whose wife was having difficulty conceiving. She would say to him, 'Leave her alone for a month, and then put a pillow under her arse!'

You Can't Win!

In the past when mothers did actually go into any detail about their labours, it was usually to complain about the horror of them: 'Oh, the agony I went through having you!' etc.

Being careful to avoid this tendency (I have mentioned already how my mother had frightened me with horror stories), I told Peggy – quite truthfully as it happens – that I supposed I was just

98

lucky, but that I had had more painful periods than when I gave birth to her. Foolishly, I thought no harm could come of my telling her this, but I had reckoned without the old 'you can't win' scenario for grandparents. To this day I am teased about how I totally failed to prepare her for the 'medieval torture' of her own labour. (Note to any pregnant woman who may read this: do not be alarmed; my daughter likes to exaggerate to get laughs!)

This is a chapter in which we have had to hear the good and bad about ourselves, so let's end on a cheering note. In September 1998 *Practical Parenting* posed the following question to a parent:

Q 'What's the best piece of advice you could give other parents?'

A 'Listen to everything your Mum tells you – she's usually right!'

Chapter 8

Discipline

Showing Who's Boss

One of the definitions of discipline in the *Oxford English Dictionary* is 'mental and moral training'. As we have already seen from the critical comments of parents and grandparents, this training is and always has been one of the biggest bones of contention in child-rearing. Parents seldom agree with each other about what is right for the child, never mind any tussles they may have with their own parents on the subject.

If the parents have themselves been strictly brought up, they usually tend to err on the side of indulgence with their children, and vice versa. Broadly speaking, and quite logically, most parents seem to react against what they consider to have been detrimental in their own upbringing, and only to adopt those rules they judge to have been fair and right.

'I used to suffer so terribly at the hands of nannies and
childminders that I made up my mind I would never ever
leave my children for others to look after,' declares a poor,
exhausted mother of three.

'My mother had no life of her own and took out her
frustrations on us. I was determined to combine having a
family with my work,' gasps a frantic professional woman –
phone in one hand, potty in the other.

'My mother was so strict with us. She would hit us with
whatever she had in her hand. I think you can get anywhere
with them by kindness,' squeaks a young mother from
beneath a kicking, biting toddler.

'I think a bit of old-fashioned discipline doesn't do them any
harm at all. A good, hard smack settles a lot of arguments,'
blares the father of a twitching, timid brood.

All of the above are, of course, stereotypical rather than real
quotations, but you may well have heard similar opinions
voiced. Beyond the microcosm of the family, out into the wider
world of civil and criminal law, the pendulum has swung wildly
between the extremes of restriction and permissiveness. Consider the constant argument about the correct treatment for
young offenders – should it be 'short sharp shock' or 'careful
counselling'? So, with our own children, should it be a smack or
an understanding discussion of the problem? In my own lifetime
I have witnessed the worst excesses of the remnants of Victorian

discipline and of the post-sixties worship of freedom of expression at all costs.

Victorian Values

In the last decade – and probably as a reaction to post-sixties liberalism – a return to 'old-fashioned values' has begun to be advocated by some politicians and educators. This is a term which, although much ridiculed by satirists, is still taken quite seriously. In using it, people invoke some kind of golden age, when discipline was of paramount importance, and by obeying its rigidly

hierarchical rules it was thought that we could conquer the animal side of our natures and grow up respecting God, Queen and Country. Its use today suggests intrinsically flawed thinking, invoking a way of life that most probably never existed and which is now totally anachronistic in the light of the waning of formalized religion, revelations about royalty and a new awareness of global, rather than national, issues.

> *Love is a boy by poets styled,*
> *Then spare the rod, and spoil the child.*
> *Hudibras* – Samuel Butler

In our modern world the emphasis has shifted from raising 'good' children to raising 'happy' children. But can't they be good as well as happy? And don't the two often go hand in hand? Can we instil principles in our grandchildren that will make them responsible citizens and at the same time help them to become fully rounded people? I believe we can.

Fear or Respect?

The hardest thing for any parent to get right is the balance between instilling a proper respect for authority and a craven fear of it. Many people of our generation complain bitterly, and sometimes with good reason, that above all, children lack respect for their elders.

But – looking at it more positively – we 'elders' now have to work harder to gain that respect; it is not the automatic right it was in our day. As children, we were taught always to defer to an older person, which could be very annoying and felt unjust when we knew ourselves to be in the right. We were almost brainwashed into being polite at all costs, and this was not always a good thing – in fact, it was sometimes extremely dangerous.

I remember a neighbour of ours, a man in his forties, who used to do fairly unpleasant things to my 14-year-old sister, like trying to kiss her and touch her whenever they were alone together. She hated it and used to tell me about what he'd tried to do. But somehow she never dreamed of telling our parents, perhaps because they were friendly with him. Of course, there were no child helplines then either, so most children just said nothing and suffered in silence.

'Although I am now in my sixties and a grandmother of three, I still feel affected by the kind of schooling I had during the 1940s and 1950s. Often, in my dreams, I am back there. I passed my schooldays in a state of absolute terror, with the result that I left as soon as I possibly could with a very poor education. Officially, corporal punishment was not permitted in the school, but the teachers found easy ways round that, like hitting you over the back of your hand with a ruler, twisting your plaits upwards or throwing the wooden blackboard duster at your head. I hated the maths master with such ferocity that I used to try to put my head in the way of the duster, hoping that it would be so badly cut open that I could bleed my way to the headmistress's study and have him sacked on the spot. I remember that one day he was standing too near to the tiny electric radiator (the only form of heating in the classroom), which he always commandeered for himself. I saw his trouser leg begin to smoulder but kept quiet, literally praying that he would go up in smoke before my eyes. But then, just as the material caught alight, one of the other girls shouted out, "Mr MacGregor, your trousers are on fire." He was a tyrant, as were most of the teachers, and that fear of authority has remained with me all my life. I only have to get ticked off by a traffic warden or some other official person and my heart pounds and I feel tears in my eyes – so I usually avoid confrontation. As a result, I tried to bring up my children to be assertive, especially the girls. I love to see them standing up for themselves against any petty tyrants who try to bully them; and I suppose I am encouraging my grandchildren to be the same. Better cheeky than intimidated, I think.'

Freedom

As a society we are much more child-centred than we used to be, so that in certain respects there is a lot more freedom for kids. They are given access to information that was kept from us when we were young, and they tend to be far less dogged by the details we were constantly nagged about, like dressing properly and having perfect table manners.

But other kinds of freedom have now gone. Whether it was just ignorance, innocence, or lack of media attention, our world did seem safer then. I remember that, at the age of nine or ten, we were often allowed to go off with a sandwich in the morning, not to return until teatime, so long as we went with another child. I was even permitted to go bird watching on my own (though perhaps because there wasn't another child eccentric enough to join me). Aged 11, off I went to the nearby countryside and roamed around the fields and woods and lanes to my heart's content. I came to no harm, but what responsible parent or grandparent could allow a child to do that now?

Peggy Writes

Of course there are certain rules that a child must learn to obey (like not beating the living daylights out of younger siblings), but children respond so differently to discipline that a flexible approach is surely better than 'boot camp' severity. The strictness of my mother's upbringing meant that she was careful not to inflict the same terrors on me, but she nevertheless believed (and still believes) in the importance of ruling rather than being ruled by children. She was always sunny and kind to me, but this in itself was a kind of discipline – somehow it was difficult to behave badly with her behaving so well. In raising my own children, I have basically tried to emulate her approach with me, though I think that I'm a bit less patient than she was.

In Our Day ...

It seems to be the norm that our generation feels that things were different in their day. We are apt to say things like:

'Children were much more polite then. They had far fewer toys and made their own entertainment. We only had a cardboard box and a pot-lid to play with.'

'My children went to bed at seven o'clock sharp and it was lights out and no nonsense.'

'We never interrupted our parents or made a noise when they were on the telephone.'

But let's get real. If it were true that the offspring of every successive generation are less disciplined, then children would all be savages by now. (Do I hear you say, 'Well, they are!'?)

Tellwright did as his father and uncles had done. He still thought of his father as a grim customer, infinitely more redoubtable than himself. He really believed that parents spoiled their children nowadays: to be knocked down by a single blow was one of the punishments of his generation.

Anna of the Five Towns, Arnold Bennett

Interestingly, grown-up grandchildren often remember their grandparents – even those who had been very strict with their own children – as being soft and uncritical. In most families the responsibility for discipline lies with the parents.

Emotional Literacy and Co-operation

Rather than laying down the law, parents now tend to enlist their children's co-operation, and I think that, in general, parent–child communication has improved. Parents talk freely with their children, but, more importantly, they also *listen* to the children's views, allowing sensible compromises to be reached. Most of us can remember the 'Do it!' 'Why?' 'Because I say so!' approach and just how unproductive it was, and I believe our children are right to try to nurture understanding and responsibility in our grandchildren, not just compliance and unquestioning obedience.

In Steve Biddulph's extremely helpful and amusing book, *The Secret of Happy Children*, he makes the point that as we inevitably 'hypnotize' our children every day, we may as well do it in a positive rather than a negative manner. To illustrate just how powerful adult suggestion is, he uses the example of a child whose throat wouldn't stop bleeding after a tonsillectomy. It turned out that during the operation the medical staff had been saying things like, 'not much chance of living' and 'she's in pretty bad shape.' They were actually talking about a previous patient – but quite freely because the child was under a general anaesthetic. Remembering that they had been talking in this way, the consultant ordered that the child be taken back to theatre, and this time the staff were instructed to say things like, 'Gee, this kid looks good and healthy … This kid has a nice healthy throat … She'll be healed in a jiffy and back playing with her friends!' The child recovered immediately and went home the next day.

My father had a similar experience. He was a GP at the time when the 'miracle drugs' like penicillin were just being introduced, bringing about the possibility of remarkable recovery from a number of serious illnesses. One of his patients, an eight-year-old girl, had been very ill with pneumonia, but had been given penicillin and was well on the way to recovery. But one day, on a routine check-up call, he discovered her to be in very bad shape; indeed she appeared to be dying. Making inquiries, he discovered that her very devout Catholic mother, who could not believe that her child would recover (tragically she had lost several others to the same disease), had asked the priest to come and administer the last rites. The child had woken up, seen the priest, reached the understandable conclusion, and obediently begun to die. My father sat beside her for an hour and literally talked her back to life: she made a complete recovery.

These stories can help us realize just how easy it is to make a child respond well or badly according to the messages that we write on the clean slate of their little minds. How often have you heard a mother or father say something about a child as if that child were stone deaf? It is all too easy for us to forget that children's feelings are 'more soft and sensible than are the tender horns of cockled snails' (Shakespeare, *Love's Labour's Lost*).

Ask any group about remarks made in early childhood that are still painful to recall, and I guarantee that 99 per cent will come up with plenty. I'm quite sure that my own five teenage years of anorexia dated from overhearing my mother's friend call me 'Fatima'. I wasn't in the least fat, and I'm sure now that the remark was prompted by anxiety about her own daughter's skeletal thinness, but it did unforeseeable damage to me.

Here are just some of the negative things parents – and even grandparents – have been heard to say:

'It's no use trying to get her to talk, she's so shy.'

'You're a little monster.'

'He's really jealous of his little sister. I can't leave them alone together – he'd hurt her.'

'He's the good one; Sally's a right little horror. She's a real tomboy. He'd have made the better girl.'

'Just as well she's pretty because her sister's got all the brains in the family.'

'She's a greedy little girl. She's going to get terribly fat if she's not careful.'

Steve Biddulph and other writers on child development now tend to encourage adults to avoid negatively programming their children and instead to offer clear, positive messages: 'You can do it'; 'Try again'; 'Do this and then you'll be ready to have a go at that,' etc.

There is also a growing awareness of how productive it can be (at times) to try to talk things through with children and to explain to them why they should do what we would like them to do. If we sometimes think that our children are trying to reason too much with our grandchildren and aren't being strict enough (not to mention smacking them), let's stop for a minute and think about how we may have been brainwashed by our own parents.

Paul Writes

My mother was a quite a strict disciplinarian. One memory from my childhood is the utter terror I felt when, as a very young boy, I inadvertently soiled my pants. I remember coming in and climbing the stairs to where my mother was, literally shaking with fear and sobbing. 'I'm sorry, Mummy, I'm really sorry. Don't hit me, don't hit me.' Much to my amazement, she was kind and gentle and just said, 'Don't worry, son. It doesn't matter. Don't upset yourself.' I think that she suddenly realized and was shocked by how frightened I was of her.

I should hate for either of my grandchildren to feel as afraid of me as I sometimes was of my mother. To be truthful, I don't find myself being all that much of a disciplinarian with Sky and Biba because most of the time we are playing games and having a pretty rollicking time. But I have to be a little careful when I'm tired because then my patience more easily runs out. Once I flared up at Sky when he was being naughty and he looked a bit upset. I felt terrible, but two minutes later he was laughing again, so I hoped my sternness may have done more good than harm!

It's a good idea to try to find out as much as you can about the parents' rules with the children and to stick to these as far as possible – particularly when you are in the parents' house. So long as we don't overstep the mark, parents are usually quite good about putting up with the little indulgences we allow our grandchildren – I think they realize that these are grandparents' perks!

In fact, when they have sole charge, most grandparents seem to have little problem establishing clear rules as to acceptable behaviour. Children are surprisingly logical and will often readily accept from grandparents such edicts as, 'No, we don't eat watching the telly in our house. We all sit at the table.' 'We don't take any drinks near the computer because they might spill on it and then we couldn't play *Topsy and Tim*, could we?' You *may* find that you have a major tantrum on your hands, but in the main grandchildren seem to accept different routines when under their grandparents' roofs.

Through quiet observation of the parents, notice what does and doesn't work with the children. If the parents' tendency is to explain things calmly and logically, then try to adopt the same approach. If the parents put a tantruming child in another room for a while to cool off, you might do the same, but be careful because little ones often seem to get more upset when a grandparent imposes a punishment (probably because they are not used to it). If the parents use a little gentle bribery, then you can probably follow suit, but try not to up the ante!

One grandmother, who lives with her daughter's family, has an extremely nice but stroppy five-year-old granddaughter. To try to tackle the little girl's habit of whingeing and tantruming she instigated a system of points for good behaviour that – like supermarket reward points – were clocked up and could eventually be redeemed against a longed-for toy. This seemed to work like magic for a day or two, but then her granddaughter started arguing the toss over how many points she had earned and the grandmother found herself spending a fortune on Barbie dolls that she didn't approve of the child having in the first place. So be very careful. Bribery can backfire on you. Perhaps the only really safe kind is what one might call activity bribery: 'If you stop whingeing right now, then we'll go to the park.' (This is especially painless if taking them to the park was what you had intended to do anyway.)

Consistency

Try – and this is a hard rule that I have myself broken many times – to be consistent in your disciplining of the children. It is only too easy to say 'No. No. No. No. No. No. No. No. No,' then – after another minute of heart-rending screaming – 'Yes, *OK* then.' Caving in is unavoidable sometimes, but nevertheless a sure-fire way to confuse the child and encourage worse behaviour next time.

Young children have much more stamina than we have for keeping up the pressure, so be prepared! One tactic that sometimes works is to distract the child before the issue becomes too intense. For instance:

Child: Gran, can I have a chocolate biscuit?

Gran: You've just had one, dear.

Child: But I want another one.

Gran: I think you've had enough for now.

Child: (face beginning to redden) But I want one!

Gran: (looking out of the window) Gosh, there's Percy (the cat)! He seems to be stuck in that tree. Shall we go and rescue him? (The child isn't tall enough to see whether the cat is in the tree or not, but the grandmother knows the cat is in the garden and that the child adores the cat. By the time they have put on coats, she can pretend that the cat has come down of its own accord, and – once outside – the chocolate biscuit request is likely to be forgotten.)

Of course, with the unpredictability of children (and grandparents), there is the alternative scenario:

Child: Gran, can I have a chocolate biscuit?

Gran: You've just had one, dear.

Child: But I want another one.

Gran: I think you've had enough for now.

Child: (face beginning to redden) But I want one!

> **Gran:** (looking out of the window) Gosh, there's Percy! He seems to be stuck in that tree. Shall we go and rescue him?
>
> **Child:** No, I don't care. I want another chocolate biscuit. I WANT IT! Aaaaargh! (Child goes purple, falls to the ground and drums his heels on floor.)
>
> **Gran:** Oh, all right then, just one more and that's it.
>
> **Child:** AAAAARGH! No, I want lots more! I want the whole box! Etc.

In an 1871 copy of *Punch Magazine* I see that even the Victorians had the same problems, in spite of their 'values'. One cartoon shows a little girl holding out her plate to a woman seated at table. The caption reads:

Grandmama: 'Candidly, don't you think you've had enough cake, Ethel?'

Ethel: 'I may *think* so, Grandmama, but I don't *feel* so.'

In such cases, Steve Biddulph recommends what he calls the 'soft-no' approach. If you find yourself losing in the battle of wills with a small child, you just start saying 'No' softly but firmly. As the child increases the pressure, you consciously relax your body and say 'No' again – but you don't raise your voice and therefore don't become involved in a shouting match. Children are too apt to win these!

Chapter 9

Eating

Crisps, Chips and Chocolate!

The issue of eating often threatens good relations between grand-parents and parents. It can start right at the beginning with the bottle-feeding versus breastfeeding debate. In my view, it is best for grandparents to stay out of that, and simply to back up the parents' own decision. I have to ignore the mostly unspoken criti-cism of my contemporaries when they discover that my daughter is still breastfeeding her two-and-a-half-year-old daughter. There is a great deal of ignorance about the subject, and I have to admit to having half-believed the old wives' tale that if the mother goes on breastfeeding for too long it may have terrible effects on her health and on the psychology of the child. Today, the idea of breastfeeding older babies and young children is finally gaining more widespread acceptance:

> *Toddlers can find breastfeeding a great support in this*
> *new, large world that they have discovered. Breastfeeding*
> *is of nutritional value, and you are still passing across*
> *many vital antibodies to your child, even if you are*

breastfeeding only once or twice a day. There is no need to stop unless you want to.'

The National Childbirth Trust Book of Pregnancy Birth & Parenthood

Picky Eaters

Many mothers wryly observe that their children will eat more with their grandparents – especially their grandmothers – than they will with them. (It is therefore worth trying to feed your grandchildren healthily.) This tendency is probably due to the fact that with grandparents there is less of a power struggle about food. Modern books on childcare are fairly consistent in advice they offer about handling problem eaters. Basically, if a child won't eat a meal, they suggest that one shouldn't communicate anxiety about it. As Deborah Jackson has said:

Assertive toddlers know that there is nothing more likely to get mother worked up into a frenzy than refusing to eat.

Deborah Jackson, *Do Not Disturb*

The Wrong Way: Eating Games!

This is all very well, but it is extremely difficult for parents and grandparents not to worry if a child refuses food, especially if that child is prone to ailments of any kind. I have to put my hand on my heart and own up to starting an eating game for my grandson, who is reluctant to devour anything but Marmite toast and chips. To encourage him to eat, I invented a naughty little boy called

Edward who throws his food on the ground, has tantrums and generally behaves abysmally. I get Sky to 'show Edward' how to do all sorts of things: eat up his fish, drink his milk, not eat the whole packet of biscuits, etc. I, of course, have to act out the roles of Edward having the tantrum and me telling him off – very sternly. Children seem to like nothing more than seeing a grown-up telling someone off other than them. I'm not sure that my daughter and her husband approve of this game, and I am quite sure that none of the child-behaviour experts would, but, heigh-ho, it sometimes gets the meal down him, the drink drunk, and means that there is a biscuit left for me.

Your lobster, sir.

The Right Way

Some children have no problems at all with eating, but others are so picky that they react to healthy food as if it were part of a fiendish plot to poison them. It helps to have healthy snacks pre-prepared (NOT chips, I hear my daughter cry!) for when they run in starving after active play, otherwise they are apt to fill up on rubbish. And you might try doing as the books advise: not fussing, not playing games (like me) or having endless conversations about eating. It seems best just to leave the food near the child and to quietly remove it if it becomes obvious that it is not going to be eaten. If (amazingly) it is, then don't go over the top with your praise either. Just stay cool!

'My husband and I are both doctors and we have always rather prided ourselves on having regular at-the-table meals for our three children and insisting that they eat everything on their plates. Recently, we had friends staying whose children were really picky eaters. We couldn't help feeling rather smug and at some length we explained our approach to our friends: very few between-meal snacks; meals served without much comment; no choices given and, if anything is uneaten, then no replacement provided. Our friends seemed very impressed, if slightly daunted. They said they were going to try to do the same and we warned them that you have to keep your nerve and persevere. The next day, however, our friends looked much happier – in fact, they seemed quite ecstatic about something. We thought they were going to show us a plate cleaned by a newly trained

child, but instead they led us to the window-seat beside the
dining table. They opened the lid. Inside were heaving,
mouldy-blue mounds. These turned out to be discarded and
rotting Brussels-sprouts, broccoli-tops and other healthy
green vegetables. Our children had revealed to their children
how to keep us happy while only eating the things they
liked!'

'You Were a Great Little Eater'

Try not to depress parents of picky children with tales of how well
they themselves used to eat, as you've probably forgotten how
often you used to finish up their leftovers. Nor is it wise to remind
them how well you cooked for them – we didn't have conve-
nience foods and microwaves when they were young, otherwise
we'd probably have used them! Talk with other grandparents and
you'll no doubt hear horror stories that will make you feel better
about *your* grandchild's particular food fads. One little boy I heard
about refused to eat anything – *nothing at all* – except Mars bars
(and he seemed fine).

It may also be a good idea not to keep cooking things that a faddy
child isn't used to. Usually it is just a waste of your time, and you
risk making them more faddy still if you keep presenting unusual
food. Children tend to be very conservative in their eating habits,
and it's probably better not to challenge this bias too much. After
all, their day-to-day nutrition usually isn't your responsibility, so
it's hardly worth getting yourself (and them) into a tizz over the
odd meal.

Nor is it wise – because you think they must be starving having eaten so little broccoli – to fill them with all the things they shouldn't have. Use your common sense about this, though. A cross, hungry child is usually better off eating a croissant instead of toast (rather than nothing), but don't stoke him or her up with iced buns and chocolate if you can help it. Quite apart from these lacking nutritional value, you need to think of their teeth. If milk teeth rot, there can be problems with those that follow.

My daughter recalls her little boy, Sky, coming home from a walk with me and announcing triumphantly, 'Mummy, I got Smarties!' I did not know that Smarties were a complete obsession of his, though – and perhaps because – he had never been allowed to eat them. In my own defence, I have to shop him now. He had chosen them, telling me, 'These are the sweets I have, Nan!' Toddlers can be very cunning, so be prepared! Also, be prepared never to get it entirely right as far as the parents are concerned. 'Twas ever thus, but you may take comfort from Dr Christopher Green's words of wisdom:

> To ensure a good relationship, the rules have to be set down, and both sides have to accept that the other has rights. When the child is in the care of the parents, then the parents are in charge of the show, and though advice may be tactfully given, it does not need to be accepted. When the grandparents are looking after the child, then they are in charge and should not be forced to adhere to the parents' often obsessive and irrelevant ideas. A child is a chameleon, who can match in easily with an ever-changing environment.
>
> Dr Christopher Green, *Toddler Taming*

It can be very irritating for parents when grandparents persist in suggesting they try all sorts of foodstuffs they know their child would be as likely to consume as pigs to fly.

First Foods

There is no hurry to start a young baby on solids. Milk – particularly breastmilk – provides all the nutrition a baby needs for the first four to six months of life. It is now thought that to introduce solids before four months is inadvisable on a number of health grounds, and that after four months the decision should be made to introduce solids on the basis of the individual baby's requirements. When the baby starts to need more feeds, wake more frequently, or reach out its hand or show an interest in food, it may be time to introduce some first tastes. Obviously you will want to take the lead from the parents on when and what the baby tries, but you might consider the following 'old reliables'.

SIMPLE PURÉES

- Baby rice
- A runny purée of starchy vegetables, like potato, sweet potato, parsnip and carrot (alone or in combination)
- A runny purée of well-stewed apple or pear (or both)
- Very ripe puréed banana (though don't try this first as it can be a bit indigestible)

These first foods shouldn't be introduced all together, just in case the baby has an adverse reaction to any of them – it's wise only to start combining foods you know agree with the baby after he or she has been on solids for a month or so. And if you are thinking of introducing a new food, do ask the parents first. First feeds can be quite an emotional business, and the parents may want to be the first feeders. There are also a few foods that young babies less than six months old should definitely *not* be fed, even in puréed form.

FOODS TO AVOID

- Nuts, which can cause very severe allergic reactions (whole nuts should probably be avoided until at least aged five, as they can cause choking)
- Sesame seeds and sesame products
- Cow's milk, cheese and yoghurt
- Wheat, rye, oats and barley
- Fish
- Eggs
- Paté
- Citrus or berry fruits
- Spices, salt, sugar
- Tea

Feeding Baby

You can use a shallow plastic weaning spoon or even the tip of your finger (washed!) to offer first feeds, and, unlike bottles, weaning dishes and spoons don't need to be sterilized, only well washed in hot water and rinsed. Don't feel frustrated if the baby doesn't seem interested, and never try to force the food in. Just follow the baby's lead, and if that means only half a spoonful at one meal, so be it. A few spoonfuls are all a baby is likely to eat when just starting solids.

'My mother has pet theories about what my toddler should eat. She's always saying things like, "He must have oatmeal and fish for his brain" and "I've just read somewhere that avocados are really good for children." But when we go out with him it's a different story. She doesn't seem to realize all the things that can't be mentioned without triggering off tantrums. In the park he can be playing happily away and she'll say, "Shall we go to the café? I'm dying for a cup of tea, and I expect you'd like a doughnut wouldn't you, William?" This to a child who would live on doughnuts if he could and is never content just to eat one. When he goes to stay with them, she reports to me, "He was an angel all weekend. He didn't have any tantrums at all, in fact he never even cried once." "Of *course* he didn't!" I feel like saying. "Because all weekend you and Dad have given him *exactly* what he wants: doughnuts, chocolate, chips, etc., and haven't even tried to make him do anything or eat anything that might be good for him." Oh, I know they love him and I really appreciate their having him, but in their reports of his good behaviour there is just an underlying hint of "You see, *we* know what's best for him. He doesn't behave badly when he's with *us*."'

He's always a little angel with me....

Peggy Writes

My son, Sky, is the classic faddy eater. He doesn't like moist food, so this rules out just about everything except chips, bread, breadsticks, biscuits, popcorn and dry cereal (and he seems to have no trouble with chocolate and sweets). As parents we've really tried every foodstuff and every approach under the sun, but even if forced to eat a fish finger – the 'eat it or else' approach – he just reverts to the usual repertoire afterwards. There is no question of him wanting anything except those specific foods. Nor is it the case that he's different with my mother. I'd happily let her take charge of his menu if I felt he'd eat a healthier diet, but she's tried all the

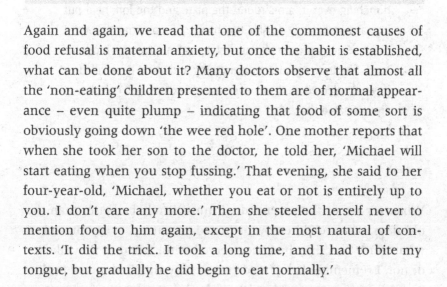

tricks in her book too and I think he's got the better of both of us. But, as she says, the more I fuss, the less he'll eat. Now we're just hoping that sitting watching the other children devour a school lunch will open his mind to the possibility of eating a wider range of foods.

Again and again, we read that one of the commonest causes of food refusal is maternal anxiety, but once the habit is established, what can be done about it? Many doctors observe that almost all the 'non-eating' children presented to them are of normal appearance – even quite plump – indicating that food of some sort is obviously going down 'the wee red hole'. One mother reports that when she took her son to the doctor, he told her, 'Michael will start eating when you stop fussing.' That evening, she said to her four-year-old, 'Michael, whether you eat or not is entirely up to you. I don't care any more.' Then she steeled herself never to mention food to him again, except in the most natural of contexts. 'It did the trick. It took a long time, and I had to bite my tongue, but gradually he did begin to eat normally.'

Often toddlers will fill up on milk and therefore have very little appetite for solid food. If you save the milk for after a meal, you may well find that your grandchild eats better. Cutting down on snacks between meals is also a good plan too, though with a picky child one is often only too happy if they eat anything at any time. The secret seems to be to try to harden your heart a little and think in the long term rather than in the short – although no one is pretending that overcoming faddy eating is easy for parents or grandparents.

Paul Writes

I suppose one good thing about having been at 14 different schools (my father was in the Air Force) was that I never had the chance to become picky. Meals at most schools were fairly meagre, and just to get enough to eat was a bit of a battle sometimes. At one school the food was so ghastly that any dish that was even faintly edible had to be guarded by hunching over it, arms round the plate and the fork held out like a sword ready to jab the hands of potential thieves. I don't remember ever daring not to eat any of my mother's food. She took ages to cook anything and she'd have killed us if we'd rejected it. I ate everything, except her coleslaw. I always hated that.

Whatever we or the parents do, it must surely be better than the old days when children were forced to eat up every morsel of whatever it was they had been served with, whether they liked it or not. I remember being made to eat cake that had mixed peel in it and having to go and be sick in the loo. My mother told me in horrifying detail her father's treatment of her brother's childhood aversion to porridge, and how it was dished up to him – meal after meal – until, out of sheer starvation, he had to eat it, often throwing up afterwards. As a grown-up he had difficulty even watching anyone eat porridge, so it certainly didn't cure him of his distaste for it.

Over-eating

There seems to be much less written about children who eat too much than about the ones who eat too little, and yet obesity in the young is an increasing problem in the developed world. It is said that what America does today, Britain will do tomorrow. If this is true, then we should be very aware of the danger of our children becoming significantly overweight. On a recent visit there, I was appalled at the amount of obese children I saw. I shall never forget in one 'diner' an enormously fat toddler who appeared to have been stuffed into a highchair that quite literally could hardly contain him, while his two doting parents took turns to spoon huge amounts of a concoction of cream, jelly and ice-cream into his eager mouth. At one point he demurred, seeming to have had enough, but the mother said, 'Go on, now, just a little bit more' and eventually spooned the whole lot down his throat.

Witnessing this was really alarming and has made me more aware of the tendency starting here. When I was young, in the forties and fifties, food was scarce because rationing went on till 1953. One very rarely saw a fat child, but now it seems all too common. There are many contributing factors to obesity in children, genetic as well as dietary, but there is no doubt that an over-consumption of junk food is one of its main causes. The car-culture doesn't help. Many children hardly walk anywhere anymore, and generally take far too little exercise. It is all too easy for them to become junior 'couch potatoes', consuming large quantities of food while watching television.

Some nutritionists advise against letting children eat while viewing on the basis that they can come to associate watching with consumption. But in general, advice about how to deal with an

overweight child is offered tentatively, because health profession-
als are concerned that giving a child a 'thing' about their weight at
an early age can possibly exacerbate eating disorders later on.

But you can, of course, try to set a good example by eating
healthily but not greedily yourself. If children are used to watching adults 'pig out', they tend to follow suit. Nor is the total denial
of fun foods for the family a good idea because 'stolen fruit tastes
sweeter'. The best approach to improving a child's overall diet
seems to be gradually to reduce the amount of sugary, fatty foods
consumed, and – equally gradually – to replace these with tasty
but more healthy substitutes. Happily, schools are now becoming
more health-conscious, with vegetarian and salad options, grilled
and baked food replacing the old-fashioned fried fare.

A word of comfort: very few of the grandparents I've talked to
seem entirely happy about their grandchildren's diets, and yet, on
the whole, children are taller and seem healthier now than they
were when we were young – so perhaps we are getting ourselves
all steamed up about nothing.

Chapter 10

The Night Shift

But I'm Not Tired ...

We've already touched on various approaches to 'putting the baby down', and heard such grandparently remarks as, 'You were always bathed and in bed by 6.30 p.m.' Often we grandparents think that we know best about how to get children to sleep at night (and all night), but that is probably because we have simply forgotten all the sleeplessness we endured as parents (in the same way that it is difficult to remember pain). I don't know of any parent who hasn't, at least for some period of their child's early years, suffered from disrupted nights. Most children don't settle into a regular and reliable sleep pattern until they are about four or five years old.

Sleeping Alone

Reading a parenting magazine some time ago, I noticed with astonishment an article about sleep problems in which a mother says, 'I tried the method of controlled crying with Sam when he was ten months old, and it worked quite well, reducing the number of times he would wake from four or five to one or two.'

I blinked my eyes in disbelief. What, is everything coming full circle again? 'Controlled crying' – the idea of letting the baby cry for a short period of time before going to it – is a version of the basically old-fashioned notion of training a baby into good sleeping habits. Are the gurus advocating it once more, after mothers being told that it is always advisable to lift their babies at the first squeak – and even to have them in bed beside them?

Peggy Writes

I know of some grandmothers – and of some parents for that matter – who think 'controlled crying' works wonderfully, but I'm so glad that my mother didn't suggest that we try it. The sound of my children sobbing absolutely horrifies me and I feel I have to attend to them immediately – it is a very strong instinct that I just can't override. Luckily, my mother has a similar response, so there isn't any tension on this score. Paul used to suggest that I needn't actually run to them, and he was right. But all along, my mother and Paul have taken the lead from us and supported our choices. I don't think they really agreed with the children being in our bed for so long, but were prepared to accept the idea because it was our decision.

The notion that it is beneficial for children to sleep alone was first engendered in the Victorian era. The argument for such a practice was expressed thus:

> Sleep habits also have to be rigidly controlled, with 'no nonsense' tolerated from the baby no matter how young ...

> The Baby Must Sleep Alone: A baby from the first should lie alone in a crib or bassinet ... It breathes purer air when lying alone. Many a child when sleeping with its mother has been suffocated by 'overlaying' ... The exhalations and breath of an older person are more or less injurious to the health and vigour of a growing infant ... A child is much healthier sleeping in the dark ...

Dr Arthur Allbutt wrote this in 1873. To be fair to him, I suppose there were other than disciplinary issues contributing to his opinion. He had witnessed many ills arising from crowded family beds: children 'overlain' by drunken parents, incest, and the spread of infectious and contagious diseases. In some cases children themselves were drugged so that they would not disturb other members of the family.

So, in the crowded, unhygienic conditions in which many Victorian families lived, with diseases such as diphtheria and tuberculosis rife, it may well have seemed healthier for a baby to sleep on its own.

Once established, the belief in the benefit of solitary and regulated sleeping remained unchanged. After all, it was so much more convenient for the parents. Here a 1930s medical officer, Hilda M Halliday, reports:

> Bedtime is another fixed hour. Up Mary goes whether she wants to or not. She's popped into bed, out goes the light, and down comes her mother. Baby doesn't always go off at once, but she isn't accustomed to being 'got to sleep'. She just lies in the dark and sings to herself.

By the 1940s little had changed, and for the next two decades the advice of Dr Benjamin Spock was representative of prevailing thought on the matter of infant sleeping:

> It is preferable to get your baby used to the idea that he always goes to bed and to sleep right after a meal. An occasional baby won't fall easily into this pattern and will go on being sociable after his meals. I'd try to change

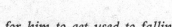
*his mind. It is good, too, for him to get used to falling
asleep in his own bed without company ...*

One might imagine that by 1967 opinions would have been
beginning to alter, but in that year Claire Rayner wrote (in *101
Key Facts of Practical Baby-Care*):

> *Not all mothers realise how early a baby discovers how to
> manipulate his parents, but there is no doubt that a
> bright six-month-old baby can soon discover that persis-
> tent crying will often bring his mother to his side in a
> hurry. Obviously he likes this, and, unless his parents are
> on the look out for this sort of behaviour, can establish a
> tyranny that is very hard to break. So, as long as you are
> sure that your baby has had enough to eat, is warm but
> not too warm, and has no pins sticking into him or any-
> thing of that sort, there is no need to worry if he cries for
> five or ten minutes after having been put down to sleep
> after a feed. Ten minutes or so of reasonable crying won't
> do him any harm at all.*

This is exactly the opinion that my generation of women grew up
with – and which seems to be staging a comeback in the shape of
'controlled crying'.

'My first baby, born in 1964, was for the first two years of her life brought up in the West Indies and slept in a cot in her nanny's room (who slept in a bed beside her). I would much rather have been in the nanny's place, but my husband was rather jealous of the baby, so I felt I had to keep him happy too.

'On the nanny's night off, he insisted that it made no difference and that our daughter should sleep in the room by herself. One evening, she started to cry. I got up to go to her and he said, "Are you just going to give in to that child over everything?" I sat down again. It was torture to hear her crying grow louder and louder. Eventually, I could stand it no longer. "I'm going up to her," I said. We quarrelled about it for a moment longer and then he slammed out of the house. I ran up the stairs full pelt, only to find that my poor daughter had pulled the mosquito net into her cot and was wound up in it like a cocoon. She was terrified and covered in sweat. As I soothed her and bathed her gently in a lukewarm bath, I swore to myself that I would never again leave her to cry. Apart from being cruel, it can be dangerous. How can we know why the baby is crying without going to check?'

Bedtime Warmth and Safety

In the last few years there has been a great deal of publicity about cot death and the connection with bedding and sleeping positions. Happily, cot deaths are very rare, but nevertheless, as grandparents, we must be aware of the risks and follow up-to-date advice on how best to lessen the danger for our grandchildren. So, here are some ideals:

- The baby's room temperature should be between 18 and 20°C (65 and 68°F).
- The Moses basket, carrycot or cot mattress should be new and not handed down from another baby (or even from sibling to sibling). It should be modern, from a reputable maker, clean, have ventilation holes at the head end and not be covered with a plastic sheet or polythene packaging.
- The sheet should be of a natural fibre and either fitted or well tucked in.
- Cot bumpers, if used, should be properly secured top and bottom and have no trailing ties.
- For a baby under a year old, use a sheet and cellular blankets rather than a cot duvet.
- Don't use pillows, however slim.
- Put the baby to sleep on her back – this is important.
- Have a night light or dim light on so that you can easily check on the baby – and check quite regularly.
- Use a baby monitor when in another room.
- Don't overwrap the baby: in a room of 18 to 20°C (65 to 68°F), the baby should probably be in a vest and sleepsuit

with a sheet and a couple of cellular blankets. If concerned that she may be too hot or cold, feel the back of her neck, which should be neither sticky nor cold, but comfortably warm.

- Don't smoke around a young baby or put a baby to sleep in a smoky room.
- Never use an electric blanket or hot water bottle for a young baby.

This may seem like a daunting list of dos and don'ts, but it's common sense really!

Some women of my generation haven't changed in their views on the need to discipline babies about sleep, but many of us now admit to just how difficult it was to leave our babies wailing alone in rooms, and to how painful it felt to imagine ourselves in some kind of battle with a 'manipulative' infant. In my view, it went against the deepest instinct you have as a mother. 'Yes, OK,' I hear you say. 'But parents nowadays have carried it too far. They run to them at the first murmur.' Well, maybe some do, when the child would in fact turn over and go back to sleep, but surely this must be better for the child than the method we were forced to adopt. Perhaps, as in all things, there is a happy medium, such as leaving the child for a moment or two to see whether she will settle, but then going to her if her moaning becomes a cry.

Three in a Bed

In the early 1990s a theory that children should share the parental bed from birth made quite an impression on British parents. In her book, *Three in a Bed, why you should sleep with your baby*, Deborah Jackson – drawing her arguments from 'many fields: medicine, anthropology, psychology and common sense' – closely and persuasively argued the case that it is unnatural for a baby to sleep separately:

> *Helplessness is the vital condition of the human baby, because he needs to be always with his mother. His frailty is her cue to pick him up and hold him.*

> *An infant lying in his cot does not understand that his mother is just across the room ... All he knows is the panic of isolation.*

> *He [the newborn] expects warmth and movement, food and comfort, all of which are supplied at once by his mother's presence and access to her breasts. Any experience that denies him these things is horrific to him. If his mother (or an equivalent caregiver) is not there, instinct tells him she might as well be dead. If his mother is dead, then he is likely to die, too. These are the meanings of an isolated baby's cries.*

She also reports on the horrified reactions she and her husband elicit from other adults when they learn of her baby-in-the-bed practices:

We certainly had no idea about the depth of feeling our sleeping arrangements would arouse in others ... When we first told people that we slept with our baby, they gave us that look. The 'Good-grief-I-knew-she-was-mad-but-don't-say-anything' look. Our strange nocturnal arrangement caused more whispering among our friends and acquaintances than anything we had done before.

Sleeping has been a bone of, well, not exactly contention, but discussion between us and my daughter and her husband. They had read Deborah Jackson's book and agreed with it wholeheartedly. The idea of their all sleeping together certainly seemed reasonable to me when the first child was born, and I can quite see what a sense of security it must give a child – whether breast- or bottle-fed – to sleep beside its mother and father. Apparently, our old fear of 'overlaying' a baby is quite groundless, unless a parent is either drunk or drugged. The practice is also sensible because, with separate sleeping, parents are usually up and down all night to comfort and feed the child. Apparently, co-sleeping can also help to prevent cot death, as the mother is constantly aware of the condition of her baby, and particularly its temperature.

As the child gets older and bigger, however, and another one comes along, it seems to me (old-fashioned granny that I am) that certain quite serious complications arise with the co-sleeping scenario. Rarely is there room for four in a bed, so the situation in my daughter's house became that her husband slept with the little boy of 20 months and she slept with the new baby – in two different rooms. Whilst I can appreciate that this is a rather effective method of limiting your family, I can't help feeling that it is perhaps not an ideal way of conducting a relationship. My daughter assures me that many parents now sleep with their children, and that most people will do it in the future, but to be perfectly honest, I have never met any other parents who do. Indeed, most of them react with horror when I mention it to them as an option.

One of the other points made in favour of sleeping with your children is that they will not then need a 'transitional' object, like a 'feely' blanket or a favourite toy. But perhaps there is nothing wrong with these, as they seem really to help a child to feel secure, especially in different surroundings.

> 'My daughter almost always has a difficult time putting my two-year-old grandson down. But when he's here I say, "Come on, Christopher, let's go up to bed with Teddy and Nanny will read to you." He puts up his arms and I carry him upstairs and read him a story. When I've finished he says, "Again, Nanny!" And I say "Why don't you tell it to Teddy?" and I go out of the room. Then I stand watching him through the crack of the door. He lies awake for a while chatting to his teddy and then he goes off to sleep, as good as gold. We find when we have him on our own, he does as we say and seems rather to enjoy the different routine.'

It is true that neither of our grandchildren has a toy that they take to bed with them, although sometimes we wish that they had, because one of the drawbacks of the 'three-in-bed' system is that when we look after our grandson on our own one of us has to sleep beside him. At first he sleeps quietly enough, allowing you to sleep for a while, but then he half-wakens and reaches out to fiddle with your ears, a rather painful fidgeting that can go on for half an hour or so while he dozes back off into a deep sleep. I feel like an abused teddy!

The upshot is that we take turns to sleep with him, but at our age it means that one of us is pretty tired the next day, which slightly reduces our enjoyment of his stay, not just for us but for him as well, as we sometimes don't have the energy to be constantly chasing 'monsters', enacting Bugs Bunny scenarios and playing endless games of 'What's the Time, Mr Wolf?' I must emphasize that we love looking after him, but, to be truthful, we are both looking forward to his being able to sleep on his own.

I know that other parents who don't sleep with their children also get disturbed by their children crying and wanting to get into bed with them, etc., so I suppose sleepless nights are all part of the fun of child-rearing. Luckily for me, my husband is extremely co-operative with Peggy's sleeping arrangements, to the extent of uncomplainingly moving beds around whenever they come to stay.

A Room of Their Own

Since writing the previous paragraph, my daughter has moved her son and daughter into their own bedrooms, my grandson's being decorated with Thomas the Tank Engine and my grand-daughter's with clowns and dolls (their choices). All is well at the beginning of the night because they love their rooms and are put to sleep by either their mother or father. The only trouble is that, being so used to sleeping alongside Mummy and/or Daddy, they inevitably wake several times, so that my poor sleep-deprived daughter and son-in-law play musical beds most nights. I suppose that, given time, the children will settle. The necessary transition from parental bed to lone sleeping seems to be the hardest aspect of the 'three-in-a-bed' scenario. An American grandmother of an eight-year-old granddaughter told me that sleeping was their one big problem:

'Katy has always been a night person, but she gets up easy in the morning. Only thing is she won't sleep on her own. Actually, she still sleeps with my daughter. She always has. We tried to make her sleep in her own bed in her own room a little while back, but she said to her mother, "Mom, I'm having a terrible time adjusting," so back she went. We'll wait till she wants to sleep alone. I guess it'll happen one day.'

In this case the mother was single, but one wonders what would have happened if she had acquired a partner. Maybe this was entirely out of the question because of the situation at home.

There seems to be no perfect way to arrange uninterrupted sleep for both children and adults. I couldn't wait to read Deborah Jackson's later book about parenting called *Do Not Disturb* because I was fascinated to discover whether she had experienced similar difficulties to those in my own family, now that she too has more than one child. (She had only one daughter when she wrote *Three in a Bed*.) Eagerly, I looked up 'sleep' in the index – nothing. OK then, 'bed' … again nothing. And this book just happens to be about letting go, encouraging 'relaxed parenting'.

However, on subjects other than sleep, Deborah Jackson is refreshingly honest about the lessons she has learned:

> *Only through practical experience can we learn the limits of what is and what is not possible. The only people able to avoid making mistakes are theorists without children ...*

So let us as grandparents try not to be 'theorists without children'. We'll get on much better that way and so will our children and grandchildren.

Paul Writes

I enjoy helping to put my grandchildren to sleep, though I've had more practice with the boy than the girl, who still needs her Mummy beside her. One night, I was lying with Sky, telling him a story about the train set that I had as a child. I spoke in a gentle whisper and gradually tailed off. His breathing grew regular and I was sure he was asleep, when suddenly he said, 'Gwampa, will you buy me a twain set tomorrow?' I said, 'Well, maybe not tomorrow, Sky. They cost pounds and pounds.' Silence. I was sure he was asleep this time, then he said, 'I know, Gwampa! You could use a cwedit card.'

A Few Dos and Don'ts for Grandparents at Bedtime

DO be prepared to look after a sleepless child in the middle of the night. One of the nicest things you can possibly do as a grandparent is say to the exhausted parent, 'I'll take him for a while – you go back to bed and have a sleep.' Full brownie points if you do this.

DO (and to be sexist, this advice is particularly aimed at grandfathers) remember that *calm* stories, songs and cuddles are best in the middle of the night. Many a woman

complains that rowdy games do *not* help to get the baby or toddler back to sleep!

DO co-operate with any arrangements the parents have for bedtime. Yes, it's lovely to put them to sleep yourself, but if they are more used to Daddy or Mummy tucking them up, your presence may over-excite them. Besides, just think, you can pour yourself a nice glass of wine and relax with the paper if you're not needed. 'Oh, no you can't!' do I hear a parent say? 'There's all that tidying up of toys to be done.'

DON'T, as has already been said, arrive around bedtime if you can possibly avoid it. There is nothing worse for all concerned because a sleepy child when excited invariably becomes a fretful child.

DON'T encourage the child to have too much to drink at bedtime, especially if they have just been toilet-trained. And remember that chocolate at bedtime can be a complete disaster, leading to sleeplessness all round, not to mention the rotting of tiny teeth!

Chapter 11

I've Never Seen Her in It

Children's Clothes

Babies' and children's fashion is another area that has changed enormously since our day as parents. Once upon a time – do you remember – babies wore nappy-liners, terry nappies and plastic pants that marked their plump little legs. At night they were dressed in smocked nightdresses of soft white flannel, and in winter wore socks as well.

> 'I spent the months of my daughter's first pregnancy sewing lots of little baby nighties – some of the softest flannel and some of cotton. I'm not a knitter but I'm a good seamstress. I took hours over the little pin-tucks on the bodice, which were the very devil to get right, and found out too late that babies don't wear such things any more, but are all in baby-grows. I was pretty sad as all that labour was in vain.'

For daywear, everything was woollen. Matinee jackets, little leggings, caps, mittens and booties were all knitted in matching pastel shades by fond grandmothers and friends. And the more skilful among them crocheted large, round shawls in the finest of white wools. Shetland baby shawls were so fine they could be pulled through a wedding ring. The shawl was halved into a semicircle and the baby was lain on it on his or her back. The right arm was placed across the chest, and the shawl folded round it, then the left arm, ditto with the shawl, until the baby was swaddled into a kind of sausage shape or, as the music-hall ditty put it:

> He's lying by his mammy in a wee white shawl.
> And he looks so cute and swanky
> Like a dumpling in a hanky ...

So when my daughter became pregnant, I said without thinking, 'What shall I knit for the baby?' Her expression gave nothing away. 'It's kind of you, Mum, but actually babies don't wear much knitted stuff now,' was all she said. I notice that contemporary advice does recommend cardigans for young babies, but warns parents to beware of lacy knitted ones because of the danger of tiny fingers catching in the holes.

Newborn Needs

Of course *your* expectant couple might be quite different and welcome piles of small, woolly garments, but do find out before you waste all that time and wool. Baby clothes today are almost as varied and fashionable as adult ones, and everything seems planned with ease of dressing in mind. So ... don't knit yourself silly for months only to find your efforts lie in the back of a

drawer. Nor is it wise to buy lovely but unsuitable garments, such as lots of pretty clothes in 'newborn' size. One grandmother was so thrilled to have a granddaughter – already having many grand-sons – that she rushed out and bought lots of (to use the mother's phrase) 'silly, frilly, tiny little white dresses'. Most babies grow out of the newborn size before you can turn around, and some are never in it to begin with! Newborn babies really need lots of stretchsuits, vests, cardigans, socks and/or booties. If they are win-ter newborns, they also need an all-in-one snowsuit and a warm hat; if summer ones, then a peaked cap to keep the sun out of their eyes, and that is just about it, apart from thousands and thousands of nappies. (Remember that chemist's tokens are always an acceptable present to new parents.)

149

Clothing Tips

New parents have enough on their hands simply learning to handle and dress their baby without having to fiddle with unnecessary buttons and fastenings or to bother with elaborate washing requirements. So, when choosing clothes, it's usually best just to buy the basics in machine-washable natural materials. Be careful, too, about buying pink for a girl and blue for a boy. The parents may want to colour-code the child, but then again may not! If buying in advance or if unsure about the parents' thoughts on this convention, 'sexless' colours like white, yellow and green are a good compromise. There are also many lovely patterned fabrics that are equally suitable for girls or boys. Anyway, keep the receipt, and if you've bought the wrong thing, you can change it. Try not to buy too many items in advance of the birth, as the baby will grow rapidly and the parents may prefer to receive fewer clothes more regularly throughout the first year than an entire wardrobe presented on day one.

- *Vests:* look for those with an envelope neck that is easy to get over the baby's head. Long vests that are like adult 'bodies' with poppers under the crotch are handy because they don't ride up and leave chilly midriff gaps, but can get a bit pooey in the event of nappy explosions. Ask the parents which they prefer.
- *Stretchsuits:* these are fairly standard now, with poppers down the front and upper legs. But choose cotton rather than mixed fibres or nylon and make sure that you don't

buy these too small, as they can all too easily start to pull
on the baby's toes (the newborn size will usually be
outgrown in a matter of weeks). You may choose from
plain cotton or terry towelling, with or without feet and
mitts (the mitts are to stop the baby from scratching). If
in doubt, ask the parents which they prefer. The baby
may sleep in a stretchsuit, though you can also buy
sleepsuits that are little different, though sometimes a bit
warmer.

- *Romper suits*: all-in-one short-sleeved, legless suits for
summer cool.
- *Cardigans:* usually more practical than jumpers because
you don't have to put them over the baby's head, but
don't assume that you must buy ones in wool and with
buttons. Sweatshirt material and poppers can be more
convenient. It's best not to buy cardigans far too big as
babies can feel a bit swamped and uncomfortable in thick
folds of material.
- *Hats:* woolly for winter and with a wide brim for summer.
But avoid long ribbon fastenings that could get caught
around the baby's neck.
- *Socks:* these can be worn over stretchsuit feet for extra
warmth.
- *Mittens:* Some babies hate these, but cold hands are a
common cause of babies' crying, and winter trips can be
misery if baby isn't wearing mittens.
- *Booties:* young babies shouldn't be put into anything that
resembles shoes. The most appropriate footwear is
elasticated cotton or corduroy booties that are roomy
around the toes and not too tight around the ankles.

We try not to dress the twins alike,
they have such different personalities.

- **Coat:** choose according to the season, but a warmly padded, hooded and rainproof coat is a winter essential.
- **Over-trousers:** padded trousers to go over stretchsuit legs are very useful in winter.
- **Snow suit:** these all-in-one, hooded outfits are like little, warm spacesuits, and are an immensely practical alternative to a coat and over-trousers combination.

Try to resist buying at birth clothes for two-year-olds on the basis that 'they were such a bargain and she'll grow into them'. Most mothers find that they have little room to store clothes, and often forget about those bought too far in advance until it is too late and they are outgrown. From all this you've probably gathered that the best idea is to find out exactly what the parents would like you to buy and stick to that.

Indeed, rather than your buying clothes that they are probably better able to choose, it can be wiser to put your money towards one of the larger items they have to buy, such as a pushchair. Although this is not quite so satisfying as shopping for baby clothes, it can be infinitely more helpful and really appreciated by the parents. But, whatever you do, don't try buying the pushchair yourself – they are the ones who will be using it, so need to select it themselves.

In fact, it's wise not to buy anything expensive without prior consultation. And if you just can't resist getting them a surprise, then try not to be upset if it doesn't go down too well. Always get a receipt and suggest that they are welcome to change it for something else.

Peggy Writes

One might imagine that choosing baby clothes is a simple task – but not so. The sizing never seemed right for my children. Friends and family would, understandably, buy my two-year-old son size 2–3, only for me to have to return it for a 3–4 or even a 4–5, as he has always been on the large side. Also, I can never work out the age spans. Is size 3–4 supposed to last till they are four, or five? I'm still unsure. Usually, I size the clothes by eye, which means that my four-year-old son is currently in Size 3 trousers one day and Size 7 the next, both fitting equally well. I have to admit that being given unsuitable or wrongly sized clothes is a complete pain. To avoid hurt feelings you often have to keep them – and even make the children wear them – or make a special journey to return them, receive a credit note and have to select something else, etc. We have been given dungarees with no poppers under the legs, dresses with stiff, uncomfortable collars, trousers with waist elastic that is far too strong and tight, and many, many items that cannot be put in the drier and/or require ironing. Happily, my mother and Paul are not ones to buy unsuitable clothes, but I am aware that they may not have seen my daughter Biba in the couple of dresses they have given her, simply because she doesn't seem very comfortable in them and tends to trip on the hems.

Today, through the post, pops a gloriously illustrated catalogue of beautiful French children's clothes. I quickly bin it. In town I hardly dare go into children's clothes shops for fear of spending a fortune on garments which will probably not be at all suitable. I have this impossible dream of buying my grandchildren lovely little outfits, and dressing them in them – like a little girl playing with dolls, I suppose. I can't help it, but I know it's not a good idea. Only the mother and father really know what they like to see their kids wear.

My daughter and son-in-law have very decided, and I think good, taste which I probably would not meet in my choices. Also it isn't simply a matter of taste; there are so many things one can get wrong – the obvious things like size of course – but also little details that only a parent notices, like sharp buckles on dungarees, waistbands that are ridiculously tight or the wrong kind of baby-gro (with or without mitts?).

The few things I have bought (when the urge was so overpowering that I couldn't resist it) that went down well were over-the-head stretchy bibs, pure cotton long-sleeved tee-shirts, long johns to be worn under trousers in winter, and a little woollen waistcoat to keep my grandson's chest warm. Now, however, I rarely buy them clothes as I find it better to give in other ways.

'I bought my granddaughter what I thought was a beautiful, classic little frock in navy blue cotton, with a smocked bodice. It was very expensive, but I thought it was worth it and that she would look really nice in it. I visited not long after and my granddaughter said very politely, "Thank you, Nanny, for buying me that really boring dress you bought me." I couldn't help laughing and told her she needn't wear it if she really thinks it boring – I wouldn't mind in the least. And she never has!'

Fastenings

Baby garments are also very much easier to get on and off nowadays. If you do buy anything, always bear in mind ease of dressing – especially if your grandchildren are wriggling toddlers. Happily, most children's clothes are now quite user-friendly.

Only one suggestion: the poppers on babygros can be very difficult to do up, and it is annoying to realize you've fastened them wrongly and must start again. A good idea would be for manufacturers to colour-code the central poppers under the nappy area, because if you do these up correctly, you're usually OK with those down the legs.

A fairly recent (and excellent) innovation is the use of Velcro to fasten children's shoes. Although there have been complaints in some quarters that by 'dumbing down' fastenings we are hindering our children from developing basic skills, parents and grandparents tend to love these. Let the complainers spend hours bent over trying to fasten a writhing toddler's tiny shoe buckle!

Hats and Shades

In our warming globe, sun hats for babies and young children are essential. I know it's difficult to make them keep them on, but you just have to persevere. Baseball caps are great for keeping the sun out of infants' eyes, but remember the danger of the ears and back of the neck getting burnt. There is no doubt that the very best protective headgear is a legionnaire's hat, which is just like a baseball cap but has an additional flap of material that goes right around the back of the child's head, protecting his ears and neck from harmful rays. Perfect! Older children may be prepared to wear sunglasses, but it can be very difficult to get a toddler to keep them on for any length of time.

Suncare

No matter how many Government warnings are issued about the dangers of exposure to sun, we too often see young children hatless, shadeless and unprotected from its increasingly dangerous rays. As grandparents it is important to be vigilant about protecting children from over-exposure.

- *Sun-block creams*: Be careful to buy creams of the highest factor for sensitive young skin – you can even get factor 50 these days – but if you are in any doubt, consult the pharmacist as to which product is the right one. Err on the side of over-application and apply liberally to all areas of exposed skin. Re-apply frequently and after swimming or bathing, and *do not forget* the less obvious places like sandalled or bare feet, hands, tops of ears and the back of the neck.
- *Sunglasses*: Check that they offer a high degree of ultra-violet protection and don't buy cheap ones. Better a hat with a wide brim or peak than cheap sunglasses – and remember that wearing sunglasses doesn't mean that a hat is unnecessary.

157

Sun Safety Tips:

- Position a paddling pool to be half in the shade and half in the sun, if possible. If the option is to put it in full sun, ensure that the child isn't exposed for too long.
- Be particularly careful when babies are in pushchairs and always take the sun-attachments for the buggy, even if it's dull when you set off. Make sure that the shade is angled correctly.
- On car journeys if possible put the baby's car seat on the side of the car that will receive the least sun, and use small car roller blinds to screen the sunlight. Also, when parking, try to remember to shade your windscreen, if not with a cardboard accordion shade, then with thick newspaper. To be strapped into a boiling hot car can make a child very uncomfortable and irritable.

Nightwear

Surely we grandparents are safe to buy nightwear, so long as: we know whether to buy a girl pyjamas, a nightdress or a nightshirt; we get the size right; we make sure that waistbands and cuffs are not too tight; we check that everything is pure cotton and as fire-safe as possible; and, of course, that whatever we buy bears the favourite children's character of the moment: Thomas the Tank Engine, Winnie the Pooh, etc! Woe betide grandparents who turn up with Teletubby pyjamas, only to find that their granddaughter has set her sights on a Barbie nightshirt.

Paul Writes

I love the way Peggy dresses the children. Clothes for kids have progressed way beyond anything our mothers could ever have imagined and my grandchildren always seem to be comfortably and appropriately dressed in clothes that are bright and fun – and that they actually like wearing. I am not quite as fussy as Peggy about always putting thick jumpers and coats on the children, but I am much more fussy than her about making sure the clothes they wear are aired. For quite a long while I think she was rather entertained by my obsession with this. But now I think she agrees with me about just how important it is. It's only too easy, in these days of few airing cupboards or clothes pulleys and practically no ironing, to put garments away in drawers before they are properly dry.

Clothes Wars

Toddlers can have very pronounced views about what they want to wear. I remember my two-and-a-half-year-old daughter insisting upon wearing her black velvet and lace party frock every day until she grew out of it. But it just wasn't worth battling over. The only time it's worth really fighting your corner is if the child isn't going to be warm enough or is in danger of getting sunburnt – otherwise there is no need to worry.

Remember that if children are running about they don't feel the cold as we do. My granddaughter hates wearing anything on her feet in the house and, no matter how cold it is, removes her socks and shoes. I worry about it endlessly and am constantly chafing her little cold feet in my hands, but she seems fine. For quite a while we played the 'Nan puts your socks on – Biba takes them off again' game until my back gave out and I gave in.

How Many Layers?

It's a very good idea to dress small children – onion-like – in layers of clothes that can be added and removed to suit the circumstances. The combination of a vest, a long-sleeved tee-shirt, a jumper and coat allow you to add and subtract clothes whenever you like, so as to keep the child comfortable.

If children get bolshie about putting on the extra layers you think they should wear, it can help to say, 'We are *all* putting on our jackets otherwise we can't go out.' If, subsequently, they look flushed and hot, feel the back of the neck. If it's sweaty, remove one layer. I find that quite lot of my grandparenting time consists of trying to judge how cold or hot my grandchildren are and to dress them accordingly – but I probably worry too much. My daughter says I do it to her too. I do remember her one day saying, with just an edge of asperity in her voice, 'Mother, I am 31. I think I know whether I am too hot or cold and what to do about it.' Oh, well, once a parent, always a parent, I suppose!

The Way it Was

I should think one of the reasons I dream of buying my grandchildren lovely clothes is because as children we were so clothes-deprived. I can remember exactly what my 'clothing coupons' provided and just how dull and limited these few garments were.

My summer outfit consisted of: two aertex shirts, one in pale pink, one in pale yellow, but both washed so often they looked the same kind of off-white colour; two charcoal-grey shorts with box pleats in the front (just like the ones that 'George' wore in Enid Blyton's *Famous Five* books); white cotton socks; and brown sandals with a cut-out petal pattern. That was summer. Oh, and I did have one faded hand-me-down cotton frock of my sister's, but refused to wear it.

My winter outfit consisted of one kilt (big brother's hand-me-down) and two striped jumpers, made from unravelled scraps of wool and knitted by my mother. (She called them my '10-day jumpers' because that's how long she took to knit them.) Then I had woolly three-quarter length socks and brown school shoes. That and my school uniform was it! Once we got a parcel from American friends and in it was a scarlet wool dress with a circular skirt. My sister and I spent hours trying it on in turn (although it was far too big for me) and twirling around in it to see it billow out like women's dresses in films.

Now I'm going to sound like a real old fogey, but I don't care! The thrill we got out of that dress would be difficult for children to imagine today, when kids can usually have whatever clothes they want. I don't think it's wrong that they can, but I think that sometimes they get so much that they cannot possible appreciate it.

I don't mean in terms of saying 'thank you,' but in experiencing the raw thrill of receiving something longed-for. OK, my old curmudgeon talk is now over!

Peggy Writes

Children are all so different in their approach to clothes. Some of the under-fives we know are already choosing what they wear each day and showing marked preferences for one item over another. Strangely, my children aren't like that at all. Sky wouldn't notice if you put him in a fluorescent dress, and Biba has no qualms about wearing a cast-off Thomas the Tank jumper with new pink velour trousers. Maybe they are just taking the lead from their grandmother. I have always teased Mum that she'll just throw on any combination of clothes that comes to hand in the morning and, although that is not strictly true, I think that as a family we are more interested in clothes being convenient and comfortable than in appearing smart and chic. Neither my children nor my mother put any pressure on me in this respect, but I must say that seeing other people's children wear perfect little outfits day after day can make me feel a bit ashamed of dressing my children in such an ad-hoc manner.

Haircuts

This seems to be an emotive subject amongst grown-ups. My daughter said she was really nervous the first time that she had her son's hair cut short, not for herself, but because she thought I might be really upset. But I wasn't at all – I thought he looked great. Older, yes, but great.

These are just some of my family's experiences. Every family has a different dress (and hair) code and you must feel free to follow it.

Chapter 12

Bottom Bits

'Darling, She's Done a Poo ...'

As I have said elsewhere in this book, one of the kindest things you can do for the parents, if they are willing, is to change the baby's nappy. Watch them, find out exactly how they do it, and away you go. No, not out of the house, but down on the mat with the baby! Though it may sound peculiar, this is actually rather a nice and bonding ritual. You take an uncomfortable child, remove the cause of her discomfort, clean and freshen her, and immediately you feel closer to her. Changing time offers a good opportunity to play and talk to the baby, and to let her kick about before the nappy goes back on.

Occasionally an infant will object vociferously to having a nappy changed, so if you've got someone else around – like Grandad – let him entertain the baby while you get on with the bottom bits. Or vice versa, of course.

'I once had to take my one-year-old granddaughter, Rowan, on an aeroplane – alone, because her mother was ill. I had been promised a seat with extra leg room, but the stewardess apologized and asked whether, as they had families with much younger babies, I would mind sitting with my grandchild on my knee. I hadn't much choice, so agreed. All went fairly (if uncomfortably) well, except that the altitude obviously bothered Rowan's ears and she cried for a while. The ultra-cold businessman on my right was clearly disgusted and made no attempt to hide his displeasure. She was quiet at last but suddenly I smelled a familiar odour that meant one thing: POO! I went up to the front of the plane with the baby and the changing bag, but all of the spaces were occupied and my darling was becoming really fretful. Oh, well – nothing for it – I realized I'd have to change her on my knee. Apologizing to the man on my right, whose eyebrows by now formed a line over his nose, I quickly and deftly accomplished the change and disposed of the dirty nappy into a passing garbage trolley. Not long afterwards, the meal trays arrived, and the stewardess kindly took the baby to let me eat my dinner. During the meal, I don't know what made me glance down but, to my horror, I saw, resting just beside the businessman's shiny black shoe, a perfectly formed sausage shape. Cold with anxiety, I pretended to drop my napkin, bent down and managed to scoop up the offending object. Holding it on my knee, I waited till the trays had been removed and then, apologizing to the stewardess who had been about to return the baby to me, I rushed to the toilet. It wasn't until I was shaking out the contents of the napkin into the loo that I

realized what I had been smuggling so carefully. It was a
sausage that had obviously dropped off the businessman's
plate. I had gone through this trauma for nothing!'

To Dispose or Not to Dispose

During this decade terry nappies have staged quite a revival, but
for obvious labour-saving reasons they haven't yet threatened the
supremacy of disposables. Terries can work out cheaper, but there
is sometimes little in it. And the ecological arguments are also far
from clear-cut, some arguing that the washing and drying of terry
nappies may be just as harmful to the environment as the dispos-
ing of disposables. Diaper wraps – Velcro-sided pants with shaped
cloth nappies inside them – are a more modern and possibly a
more convenient alternative to terries secured with pins, but to
use them parents still need nappy liners and a bucket with lid.
With these wraps parents can usually choose to wash them themselves or have a service come to collect dirties and return cleans.

Toilet Training

When my grandson was still quite young, I bought him *The Potty
Book* with pop-ups and tabs that demonstrated the whole toilet
routine. He loved tugging the tab that pulled the little boy's
trousers down to reveal his bare bottom, and the one that made
the wee-wee appear to pour into the loo. My daughter was quite
amused by this purchase as she thought it would be ages before

he could copy the protagonist of the story. But I have to say the book was a great success, not just in helping *him* to enjoy the whole idea of sitting on the potty, but also his little sister, who still says, 'Help! Quick! I need my potty,' when she does. The book is still popular with them now, though almost completely tab-less.

Children and 'Bums'

Depend upon it, your grandchildren will – like all children before them – be fascinated and amused by anything to do with bottoms, poo, wee, willies, etc. Talking of the word 'willy' (a euphemism now almost universally adopted by parents), parents are often at a loss as to what to call their female children's genitalia. Despite our liberated age, there is a general squeamishness about this that must, I think, stem from the old-fashioned denial of female sexuality. As children we were forced to refer to 'front bottoms' and 'back bottoms', and I have a clear memory of my mother's shocked face as she found me, aged about three, rubbing soap into my 'front bottom'. 'You mustn't do that,' she said, 'You'll hurt yourself.' I remember feeling very puzzled, as it had only felt rather nice to me.

'My mother-in-law was extremely shocked the other night when her two grandchildren were getting ready for their bath. She doesn't get to be with them that often, and she was waxing all dewy-eyed about "seeing my two little cherubs having a bath together". I quite forgot to warn her about their current game in which my four-year-old strips himself naked, invitingly protests, "No, Nina, don't tickle my willy!" then runs off pursued by his giggling two-year-old sister, who catches him and tickles his willy. "What are you going to do about this?" my mother-in-law gasped, and she looked really pained when I said I was going to do nothing and it would pass like all phases. When I asked if she remembered playing bottom games when she was little, she looked ready to faint and left soon after. I'm sure she thinks we're all perverts.'

The Victorians must carry much of the blame for adults' anxiety about children's interest in their own bodies, the legacy of their prudery lasting well into the 20th century. In this exchange of letters between a mother and a grandmother of the 1920s, the writers reveal a deep fear of 'self-abuse' by children, especially boys:

My Dear Mother,

I'm very worried about a thing I discovered the other day. You know my Margaret and her little friend Terry have their afternoon rest together in their 'wigwam' in the garden. Well, one day Terry's mother and I went to fetch them in, and found they had crept away down behind the currant-bushes and were both of them doing the little business which is usually done in the private in the closet. They both seemed ashamed at being found at it, and couldn't explain why they had done it. Terry's mother told me then that Terry has a habit of pulling himself about and straining. He used to do it in bed at night till she put him into little pyjama suits, and also got him to hold tight on to his old dolly with both hands. Even now he does it occasionally. Among her husband's things after he died she found a book called: 'What boys should be told' and she read part of it and was awfully afraid that this trick of Terry's was really a vicious habit – what the book called 'self-abuse'. We are both so sure that our children are clean-minded and wholesome, and we can't really believe that they are teaching each other dirty tricks – but what are we to believe?

Write soon and tell me what you think.

Enid.

Dear Enid,

I'm glad you wrote to me about Margaret and Terry. How history does repeat itself! I suppose you don't remember the same happening when you were tiny? I left you in the charge of your brothers one afternoon and found much the same thing when I came back. But it was more of a shock to me, for they were bigger boys, about six and seven, and you were only two. Your father was inclined to be very angry with the boys but I got him to write to our old friend Dr Wise and ask his advice. We kept the letter and this is what he wrote:

'Dear Mr Hawkins, Nearly all children go through a time of being extremely interested in those parts which are sometime described as "private" just as they go through a time of being absorbed in their fingers and toes and in learning how to use them ... There is nothing vicious or unhealthy about it. Don't punish your boys, or let them feel either wicked or injured. Tell them, that it is not the sort of thing they would like any other boy to do in front of their little sister, and that knights and heroes don't waste their time at that kind of game ... You can give your little boys all the noble ideals that will make impurity impossible for them. If a boy has a big desire to be a fine man, if he has a great admiration for physical fitness, and mental keenness and moral worth, there won't be much room for the animal temptations. They will come, probably, but he will be able to say to them, "I've no use for you today, thank you." '

I've copied parts of it out for you, Enid; it puts things rather clearly and may help you and Terry's mother to think out how to divert Mary and Terry's interests into, shall we say, more polite directions.

Love, *Mother*

It's wonderful, isn't it? Such a mass of euphemisms, but I suppose, for their time, they were being quite frank to discuss it at all. It is also very apparent from this exchange that girls were still considered the innocent victims of male sexuality.

Discipline and the Bowels

In the Victorian age discipline of the bowels was attempted with babies from the moment they tumbled out into the world. Regulation and control of every natural physical function was thought to be inseparable from later control in the moral department. *Self-control* was the watchword, and was demanded of them even as infants, the acquirement of good 'habits' being drilled into them from the very beginning.

> *A child should be taught at a very early age habits of cleanliness. At least half a dozen times a day a little pan (warmed) should be placed under the infant as it lies on the lap, by which means it may be taught, at three or four months of age, to dispense with napkins.*
>
> *Every Mother's Handbook*, Dr Henry Arthur Allbutt

This is quoted from a Victorian childcare manual of 1897. Even the author's name, Dr Henry Arthur Allbutt, has the correct Victorian ring!

Just in case you think such practices went out with the old queen, listen to a mother in the 1930s:

> *Baby's kept all her good habits too. I hold her out* ['baby' is five months old] *just as nurse did, and she's as good as gold – I never get a dirty napkin.*
>
> *Letters from a Grandmother*, Hilda M Halliday, MRCS, LRCP, DPH,
> Medical Officer for Maternal and Child Welfare,
> Somerset County Council

And a child-health specialist speaks out in 1955:

Mother should try right from birth to train her baby to pass his motion into a small chamber-pot as it is a dirty, unhygienic habit to allow him to do it just anywhere and at any time …

Care of Mother and Baby, C Elaine Field, MD, MRCP

Toilet Training Now

Luckily, such attitudes have not survived. Sometimes grandparents are heard to make slightly critical remarks about the somewhat more relaxed approach of modern parents towards toilet training, but mostly they seem to fall in with the new ideas and feel that perhaps they were a bit too fanatical about it. Different children achieve control at different ages, with girls apt to be ahead of boys. Generally speaking, most toddlers achieve full control, with occasional lapses, at between two and three, but there is no need to worry if this is not the case. But, if they are trying hard, it's a good idea to encourage and praise them because a word from grandparents can make a great deal of difference.

Never feel tempted to scold your grandchildren if they have an accident as this can happen to any infant, however fully trained. I remember being in a dancing class, aged five, and not having the courage to ask to 'leave the room'. Just as I made an elegant curtsey, I flooded the classroom floor!

When you've got to go, you've got to go.

Peggy Writes

I think the only way to train a child is to allow them a few accidents. When we thought they were ready for it – at between two and three – we just took our children's nappies off, put them into pants instead, and tried to remember to pop them on the potty every hour or so. Within a couple of days they had basically got the hang of not peeing on the carpet. Obviously, the ideal is to do this in summer, when they can be outside, but whenever you do it, don't make a fuss about the whole process. Mum and Paul seemed in agreement with our approach (I hope they really were!) and didn't bother about the odd accident that happened at their house. Of course, all children are different and what works for one doesn't necessarily work for another. But if they feel that their parents and grandparents have confidence that they can do it, and are not punished for small setbacks, then they usually succeed in becoming dry sooner rather than later.

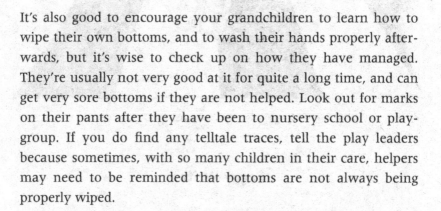

It's also good to encourage your grandchildren to learn how to wipe their own bottoms, and to wash their hands properly afterwards, but it's wise to check up on how they have managed. They're usually not very good at it for quite a long time, and can get very sore bottoms if they are not helped. Look out for marks on their pants after they have been to nursery school or playgroup. If you do find any telltale traces, tell the play leaders because sometimes, with so many children in their care, helpers may need to be reminded that bottoms are not always being properly wiped.

Paul Writes

Every single thing about our 'bottom bits' was euphemized when I was a child. The penis was a 'whistle', breaking wind was 'pipping', and, as good Catholics, we were taught that to touch yourself 'down there' was a pretty unforgivable sin. In my entire life, neither of my parents ever spoke one word to me on the subject of physical parts or sexuality. Even when I was grown up, the nearest my father could get to describing a couple having sex was, 'Oh, you know, they were ... *kissin'* and cuddlin'.' And he blushed a deep red as he said it. We were expected to be clean 'in word, mind and deed'. It is therefore with a feeling of relief and pleasure that I witness my grandchildren's open and uninhibited acceptance of their bodily functions, and applaud their parents' honest and unembarrassed attitude. I think how lucky the children are that they will not grow up associating their own bodies with sin.

Chapter 13

Developing Potential

Bringing Out the Best

As your grandchildren grow a little older you will no doubt witness the parents debating the issue of their education.

Now, here's an opportunity for you to sit back and savour being a grandparent rather than a parent, because now the decisions are not all your responsibility. My daughter laughs when I ask her, 'Is it a bisexual school, dear?' having temporarily forgotten the correct term. Although obviously I care deeply about their education and hope that they will do well at their schools, I don't have that sinking feeling that it will be my fault if they don't.

However, although the responsibility may not be yours, it is no doubt still a matter of great interest to you how your grandchildren are going to be educated and one in which you can be of great help. Grandparents are often the 'inspirers' of children. Time and again one reads of how an enthusiasm was instigated by a grandmother or grandfather – an enthusiasm that may later turn into an occupation. Children often regard their closest older relative as the fount of all knowledge and consult them about many things. Here is one eight-year-old boy's view of the importance of a grandparent:

> A grandmother is a woman who has no children of her own, and therefore she loves the boys and girls of other people. Grandmothers have nothing to do. They have only got to be there. If they take us for a walk they go slowly past beautiful leaves and caterpillars. They never say 'Come along quickly' or 'Hurry up, for goodness sake.' They are usually fat, but not too fat to tie up our shoe-strings. They wear spectacles and sometimes they can take out their teeth. They can answer every question, for instance why dogs hate cats and why God is not married. When they read to us they do not leave out anything and they do not mind if it is always the same story. Everyone should try to have a grandmother specially those who have no television. Grandmothers are the only grown-ups who always have time.
>
> Introduction to Drama Therapy, Sue Jennings

Good to know we're important! Even a more modern granny, with all her teeth, still makes the grade:

> **My grandma is my favourite friend. She is a designer. She is always very busy because she often does three jobs at once but she always has time for me. She has a studio and she**

lets me use all her paints and stuff. She never cares if I make a mess, which I do sometimes because of the glue when it gets stuck on the wrong places. The only things she's fussy about are the paintbrushes. She shows me how to wash them out really well, and the only time she was ever cross with me was when I left a brush standing in water. Then she calmed down and told me that it was made of something called sable, which is very precious, and that if you leave it standing in water you spoil all the pointy bit.

Saving for Your Grandchild

Although, when your first grandchild arrives, you won't necessarily have to think about the parents' choice of school just yet, you may feel very strongly that you want to contribute towards the child's education – whether by helping with school fees in the private system, or paying for extras, like school trips, in the state system.

To allow you to do this, you might want to set up some kind of saving plan. You can be pretty sure that any scheme you begin now will be very helpful both to the parents and to the child. My daughter's paternal grandmother put aside a little money for her, and it proved invaluable, not only in helping with her secondary schooling, but also enabling her to live abroad and learn French in the year before she went to university. It's probably the most important investment you can make. Don't feel inadequate if such a plan is beyond your means – just starting a post-office savings account for a child is a good idea, adding little amounts to it if and when you can afford them. Time passes quickly and, before you can wink an eye, that little scrap in a babygro will be a teenager needing funds!

Toys

Needless to say, these are now far more varied and interesting than in our young day when a few cherished objects were the sole possessions of most children. In the main, modern toys are excellent: stimulating, safe and educational. The only problem they present us with is one of choice, because with such an enormous range for all age groups, picking the best can be difficult. My daughter once took me to what looked like a massive toy supermarket with aisles and aisles of brightly coloured goods. I was after something educational but fun for my then three-year-old grandson, and took about an hour to choose something. In my view, it may be better to take the child with you to a reasonably sized toyshop in which the selection isn't so overwhelming. Also, do ask parents what it would be beneficial for the child to have, as some toys are clearly less worthwhile than others, and they may not, for instance, want a boy to have a police set, complete with gun.

Noisy Toys

Also beware of extremely noisy toys. It's all very well to put up with listening to drums, whistles and cymbals on Christmas Day (you'll have a sherry or two to get you through it), but imagine hearing these noises on a daily basis. Some of the battery-operated toys nowadays would drive you completely crazy – and the same goes for so-called 'musical' toys. Test it out in the shop and try to imagine what it would be like to hear it again and again.

Also, refrain from buying very loud toys for small babies, as there is a slight danger that these may damage their hearing. Even if they don't sound all that loud to you, remember that babies always hold them very close to their heads so that the volume is effectively on full.

All in all, with regard to the children's development and education, you are a very important person. You probably have more time to read to them, play with them and teach them about things than the usually rather busy parents. It may feel as though you are not doing much, sitting chatting to your grandchildren as the parents rush about organizing practical things, but you are in fact doing a phenomenally important job in encouraging their young minds – feeding their thirst for knowledge and their hunger for stories.

At Grandma (and Grandpa's) Knee

Perhaps the best thing of all about becoming a grandparent, especially if you are lucky enough to have frequent contact with your grandchildren, is the process of gradually becoming a 'major figure' in their lives – often with an almost god-like power to make them happy.

Babies and young children appear to feel the bond instinctively from the first, but later it is delightful to observe their dawning realization that you are their parent's parent. They gaze at you, and you can practically see their minds wrestling with this new concept. What? Their parents were once children like them with bossy mummies and daddies too? And *you* were those bossy mummies and daddies. Then the questions start and the requests for stories begin: 'What did Mummy do when she was little?' 'Tell us a story about Daddy when he was a schoolboy,' etc.

To make the link between past and present is an important part of our 'job' as grandparents. By beginning to fill the children in on their background – where they came from – we nurture in them a sense of what it means to be a family, and help them to make sense of their own role within it.

If your grandchildren are adopted, then it is all the more important to develop their sense of belonging. A loving grandparent can make all the difference to a youngster struggling to come to terms with the particular anxieties that the knowledge of being adopted brings.

So we are, as grandparents, in a privileged position. We are the custodians of the family's facts, myths and legends. We can tell them about when 'Mummy was naughty' – they *love* such stories – and, in the process, educate them in all sorts of ways.

Knowing that Mummy went to school and grew to like it can, for instance, give children enormous courage when they themselves have to go – and I think it is important for children to start to get a sense of their parents being rounded human beings with real histories and childhoods. Tales of 'when Mummy was good or naughty' can serve as exemplars of acceptable and unacceptable behaviour without the grandchildren even noticing the moral message of the stories.

When we sing old songs to our grandchildren and tell them rhymes that our parents and grandparents told us, we continue the particular traditions of the family. Most of the funny songs and verses I amuse my grandchildren with come not from my mother, but from my grandmother – and she was born in 1873. When I'm with them, things I thought I'd long forgotten come bubbling up from 'the dear dead days beyond recall'. For instance, I find myself playing a game that involves sitting the child facing me on my knee, and bouncing him up and down, singing:

> *My name is Jims Jones Benjamin Binns*
> *I was cut right down in the midst of my sins.*
> *For my home is down below,*
> *But when the cock commences to crow ...*
> *Fare thee well, Benjamin Binns!*

On the 'Fare thee well' I open my knees and let the child drop backwards, upside-down but still holding on to my hands.

I realize that this is a song and game my grandmother used to play with us, and that she learned it from her husband who was madly keen on the music hall. 'Jims Jones Benjamin Binns' must have been sung by some Victorian 'turn' in the character of a man who has been hanged for his sins and is now a ghost. Bloodthirsty, you might think, but none of that came across to me when I was a child. It was just a game that was great fun.

And then there is:

> *Skinny-malinky-long-legs,*
> *Big banana feet,*
> *Went to the pictures and …*
> *Fell …* [The child falls between the knees, as in the last game]
> *Through the seat.*

To which I have added:

> *When the picture was over,*
> *Skinny-malink got free* [the child is pulled back up on
>   to the knee]
> *Skinny-malink and Nan – they had a cup of tea.*
> *Cheers!* [We clink imaginary cups]

Before you condemn me as an out-and-out madwoman, just wait until your first grandchild becomes old enough to play with. I can almost guarantee that you'll come out with, and invent, games just as fantastical. You can revisit the exuberance of your own youth and – in the execrable phrase – 'Get in touch with your inner child.' As one woman, Helen Thomson, observes: 'Most grandmas have a touch of the scallywag. And not just grandmas, but grandfathers too.'

Oral History

In this visual age, it is essential, I think, not to let our oral culture die. Try to dredge up all the odd little scraps from your past and pass them on to your grandchildren. They will love it. Recently a magazine appealed for older people to write down all the funny little rhymes and skipping games they could remember, and literally hundreds replied. It made fascinating reading, sparked off all kinds of memories, and was later made into a book.

Here's a strange rhyme that my grandmother learned from her Scottish grandmother (so that takes us back to the 18th century!). This, I believe, was a skipping game:

> *A-zeenty teenty*
> *Heathery-bethery*
> *Bumpty-sugary*
> *Hovey-dovey*
> *Saw the laird of*
> *Heezalum-peezalum*
> *Jumping over Methuselah's dyke*
> *Playing on his wee-pee-pi-po-puddock pipe!*

And a variation on that for when the skipping changed rhythm slightly:

> *A-zeenty-teenty*
> *Heather-bell*
> *El-del-dod-erel*
> *A-zeenty-teenty*
> *Tarry rope*
> *Ran-tan*
> *Toozy joke!*

A Sense of Rhythm

Not only are games like these fun, they are deeply rhythmic and therefore satisfying both to say and to hear. The child can learn them quickly because of that insistent rhythm. Educators are now realizing just how important it is for children to learn nursery rhymes and to play rhythmic games in early childhood. A sense of rhythm leads to a later facility for and appreciation of all sorts of things, like music and poetry, and may also help to develop our conceptual understanding of patterns of all sorts – even improving our grasp of mathematics! So when you are playing with your grandchildren, don't dismiss as nonsense any early rhythmic fragments that may surface from your past. They are important.

Paul Writes

My parents didn't really pass on any of these fragments of verse to me, so I might have been deprived rhythmically had it not been for the fact that both of them loved dancing and singing. I was brought up hearing them sing all the ballads of their time – Cole Porter's, Irving Berlin's – and particularly Frank Sinatra's songs, the words of which my father always managed to get wrong. He was a drummer in the Air Force band, so had a great sense of rhythm – they both had. (I often think it was the only thing they had in common!) For Sky and Biba, I seem to fulfil another function, that of the character actor. They beg for me to be 'Black Dog' (a rascally but silly pirate of my own invention), Bugs Bunny (we all know him), 'Whistling Monster' (a monster who seeks them out by whistling) and all the engines in the Thomas the Tank stories. Sometimes I start off in the character of 'Black Dog' when my grandson will suddenly say, 'No, be Edward!' (The naughty boy Claire invented), and then, as soon as I have got two words out, my granddaughter will shout, 'No, Gwampa, be Pwicilla' (Priscilla, Edward's naughty little sister). So you see, as a grandfather, let alone an actor, you have to be pretty versatile!

Storytelling

I keep hearing people of my generation and younger saying things like, 'I wish I'd asked Mum about her grandfather and that side of the family. It's too late now.' Never be afraid of boring your grandchildren with stories. Most children soak up tales about their forebears with seemingly endless interest. My father wrote about his early life for my daughter, and it is good to know that we can pass to our grandchildren in the early 21st century his account of what he was doing in the early 20th century. Even now, they love me to tell them about the day my father refused to hold out his hand to be given the strap by a stern schoolmaster. They even make me enact the dialogue:

Teacher: Hold out your hand, Jack.

Jack: (*hands firmly held behind his back*) No, thank you, sir.

Teacher: Hold out your hand, I say.

Jack: No thank you, sir.

Teacher: What do you mean by it?

Jack: Well, if I hold out my hand you'll only hit it.

I would call that an early object lesson in thinking for yourself and not submitting to physical abuse, wouldn't you? Or do you take the line that he had no respect for authority? We're back to that old argument again, but as grandparents we keep an open mind – don't we?

Phone Calls

Another great thrill of grandparenting, and one you can enjoy no matter where you are, is when your grandchild first talks to you on the telephone. For months you will have been listening to the child breathing or gurgling, but then comes the magic moment when you hear, 'Hello, Grandpa' or 'Hello, Gran'.

Telephone conversations with young children are, to say the least, unpredictable. You can be in the middle of asking them what they are doing, when they run off without telling you or their parents, and, if they've made the call you are left connected and helpless until someone or other realizes the phone is still off the hook. Or they press the wrong buttons and you suddenly get cut off. Children are also apt to get a little confused about the telephone's power of communication. My granddaughter said to me the other day, 'Look at my new shoes, Nan' and my daughter told me that she was holding her foot up to the mouthpiece so that I could see her nice red shoes! Trying to hold phone conversations with the parents can also be somewhat unpredictable, as you never quite know how long you've got:

'Sorry Mum, she wants to do a poo.'

Or

'No! No! Get down from there or you'll hurt yourself. Got to go! Sorry.'

Phone slams down and you are left still wondering about all the things you had intended to ask. So motto for grandparents is Never Expect to Finish a Conversation – that way you won't be disappointed, and will learn to hone the skill of extracting and passing on any vital information in the first few minutes before the phone goes dead.

Grandchildren should be discouraged from playing about with phones. The emergency services were not amused when my then two-year-old grandson called them three times in one week. He wasn't doing it on purpose, but nine was the nearest button to keep pressing!

Peggy Writes

Before I had children and was still working in an office, I phoned an elderly art historian who often talked of his ill health. My call was answered, but instead of his calm and erudite tones I heard a terrible sucking in of breath, a low moan and an alarming crashing noise. There was no doubt about it – he had answered the phone only to suffer a massive heart attack. I called an ambulance and sat at my desk in a state of shock. About 10 minutes later, my phone rang. 'I'm not so easy to get rid of, you know,' said a hale voice. What I hadn't realized was that, loving and dutiful grandparents that they were, he and his wife looked after their baby grandson one day a week and the infant had answered the phone.

Special Relationships

The relationship between a grandparent and grandchild is a pretty special one anyway, but sometimes there can be additional affinities. This doesn't mean for a moment that you will have that forbidden no-no – a *favourite* grandchild – but there is nothing to stop you from enjoying a particular empathy with one child in one direction and with another in another. Quite regularly, though, grandparents do admit to feeling a very strong bond with their first grandchild, and worry that they might not be able to feel the same about the others. From my own experience, I think that there is no need for anxiety or guilt about this. With my own two grandchildren I did find it easier to form a close relationship with the first sooner than I did with the second. This worried me for a while, but I now realize that many factors contributed to this: the initial thrill of my new role, the fact that I saw my grandson in the hospital immediately after his birth and was around for the first few days of his life. These circumstances all helped to make me feel close to him.

With the arrival of his baby sister, we all took turns to sleep with him to help him to cope with the very natural jealousy he felt. He could no longer sleep beside his Mummy, so he needed all the love and reassurance he could get from us. The quiet intimacy of that contact brought us very close.

I have never slept beside my granddaughter, and haven't therefore had such physical closeness with her, but now that she is two-and-a-half, and a sociable, talkative little person, our relationship has become stronger and stronger. We can chat and play and she will suddenly say, 'Nan!' in the most affectionate way imaginable and throw herself into my arms for a cuddle. So allow yourself time and don't panic when you don't immediately feel the same intensity of passion about your second, third, fourth and other grandchildren. But do try not to emulate one great-grandfather, who had so many great-grandchildren that, when he was shown a photograph of the latest, was heard to mutter, 'Not another bloody baby!'

Sibling Rivalry

This is one area where you can be of enormous help to the child who is suffering the jealousy – indeed, to both children, because such rivalry is difficult for both. My grandson, when just under two, was so jealous of his little sister that when he and I were playing together and his mother brought the baby into the room, he used to yell, 'No, Mummy, take her away. I don't want her!' One day he even said, 'You can throw her away now, Mummy.' Such a situation is really tricky because you can't just give in to the jealous child and take the baby away, far less throw her away!

We all knew that, although he was so young, he did have a very good understanding of language. So whenever a crisis occurred, one of us would hold him very firmly in a cuddle, and tell him that no one could ever take his place. We told him that, though we loved Biba, we loved him as well, and tried to make him feel special because he was older. It was very difficult and took a long time and plenty of hugging, and although none of us would pretend that he doesn't still compete for attention, he is a lot better and now really adores his sister. They do a lot of kissing and cuddling, but, like all sisters and brothers, still scrap over things like who should go to bed first. Recently, my daughter explained to him that he had to go to bed first because his sister was still having a long afternoon sleep. The next day at three in the afternoon he climbed into bed by himself and put himself to sleep. That night he said triumphantly, 'Now I can stay up later than Biba, because *I* had an afternoon nap.' Children are always one step ahead of you!

The Other Grandparents

Whilst we are on the subject of rivalry, we have to remind ourselves that just as we tell children that we have room in our hearts to love more than one of them, so the children have the capacity to love more than one set of grandparents. Relationships between these two sides are therefore intrinsically loaded and must be handled with as much delicacy as we can muster. Several grandparents have confided to me that they feel more secure all round when the grandchildren are their daughter's children rather than their son's. This is natural enough, perhaps, but it is very important for the son's parents to feel that they can be as much in the picture as the daughter's. After all, what could be better for children – especially in our fractured society – than to have the full complement of four grandparents?

The whole in-law area can be fraught with tension. Who is told first of the pregnancy, the birth and the first tooth? And, later, which grandparents are birthdays and Christmases to be celebrated with? Holding double celebrations can help here, and of course grandchildren are usually more than happy with this arrangement, but it can be a bit labour- and time-intensive for the parents.

One maternal grandmother described how, in the presence of the other 'Gran', she has to keep gently pushing her grandson away from her knee to disguise his preference for her. She says that this is not the fault of the other grandmother, but simply because she doesn't get the opportunity to visit the boy so often and so knows him less well.

The exercise of tact in relation to the other set of grandparents is a delicate skill that needs practice – especially if ideas about child-rearing do not coincide. However, it's impossible to legislate for the grandchildren's affections and loyalties. Almost inevitably they have their own preferences.

It's quite a good idea to encourage children to call each grandparent by a clearly separate name, otherwise you may find yourself being referred to as 'Other Granny', which is a bit disconcerting. In my family we called my paternal grandmother 'Granny' and the maternal one 'Gwenny', and to us they were worlds apart. My grandchildren quite naturally and of their own accord have dubbed me 'Nan', whilst they call their daddy's mother, 'Granny.'

So far as getting along with the other grandparents is concerned, perhaps the best plan is to try to let any relationship develop – or not – according to how you would get along with them in an ordinary social situation. If personalities clash, then, with the best will in the world, there is no way you can force yourself to become bosom pals. I find that most sets of grandparents have a fairly distant but polite association with each other. Interestingly, I have not come across any that are the greatest of friends. It just seems to be in the nature of things. They usually don't meet all that often for one thing, and each tends to take their separate place in the lives of the grandchildren.

One word of warning: if there is ill feeling of any kind between the grandparents, don't let the grandchildren know about it. Family bonds are very special and, if it is humanly possible, shouldn't be broken. I can remember hating hearing my mother saying things about my grandfather, whom I loved dearly, although I do believe he was very difficult with her.

I didn't have much fondness for my first mother-in-law, who was apt to do things like replacing the greyish rag I had on my sink with a new white dishcloth, saying, 'I always say you can tell a real lady by her dishcloths.' She was, however, a good grand-mother to my daughter, so I tried – only my daughter can tell you whether I succeeded – not to express my dislike of her. At least not until my daughter was grown up!

What They Call Us

Sometimes children make up their own names for us. We may decide that we want to be called 'Grandmama', but they have other plans. A close friend of mine was determined to be called 'Grandy', but the nearest her grandson could get to that was 'Landy'. So she became 'Land' and her husband, who is Welsh, is called by the Welsh word for grandfather, 'Tied' – so between them they are 'Land and Tide'. Perhaps it's just as well their grandson is not called 'Sky', like mine! By the way, I can always tell what people think when I tell them his name. They either immediately say, 'Oh, what a lovely name!' with real enthusiasm, or else they smile anxiously and murmur faintly, 'How interest-ing. How unusual!'

An American grandmother admitted, slightly shamefacedly, that her grandchildren call her 'Toots-Mom'. When, intrigued, I re-quested an explanation, 'Toots-Mom' came up with a great exam-ple of oral family history. Apparently, when she was little she had been stomping about blowing on a toy trumpet. *Her* grandfather (probably driven mad by the noise) said to her, 'You're a real little tooter, aren't you?' whereupon she replied indignantly, 'I'm not a little tooter, I'm a big tooter!' Ever since that day, she had always been referred to as 'Tooter' and that's how 'Toots-Mom' came about.

Celebrations

Grandmothers, from what I've heard, often seem to be the ones who make the birthday cakes, although I know a clever grandfather who does the most beautiful and elaborate ones it's possible to imagine. If this task is one that you think you might undertake in the future, let me just whisper a word or two in your ear … be careful what kind of cake you make. My grandson ordered Thomas the Tank Engine. I knew it would be quite a task because it would have to be pretty accurate to live up to his exacting standards. But in the local cake shop they quoted an astronomical price. 'Right!' I thought, gritting my teeth. 'I'll do it myself.' I thought out ways of making it easier, like buying a chocolate Swiss roll to form the body of the engine, and ready-coloured icing sugar and icing pens. I collected all the ingredients together on the kitchen table and felt competent and confident, having the day before baked thin sponges out of which to create the other parts of Thomas. I had even heated apricot jam ready to use as cake glue.

Nine hours and many swear words later I finished Thomas. I must say, it looked really good and to see the utter delight on Sky's face made it almost worth it, but I have to admit that for his next birthday I had recourse to the local supermarket fancy cake shelves and bought him an amazing racing-car cake, which, because of the Thomas triumph the year before, he assumed that I had made myself. I felt a bit of a cheat, but I couldn't go through that again.

Christmas is naturally a wonderful time to be with your grandchildren. Suddenly the whole occasion seems worthwhile again as you fill stockings and creep about. On Christmas morning we always end up with the six of us all sitting on top of one bed in order to savour Sky and Biba opening their stockings. And on Boxing Day, off they go to their other Granny and have more presents and party-time with her.

But quite apart from any particular celebrations, I'm sure you will find most of the days you spend with your grandchildren special in all sorts of ways. You are embarking on one of the most exciting and fulfilling times of your life, and one which will last for the rest of it. I wish you all great happiness, but I don't even have to say 'enjoy it' because I know you will!

Practical Matters

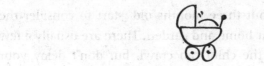

Safety in the Home

Before the Birth

It is never too soon to start thinking about the safety of your home and garden. Even before your first grandchild is born, you might want to consider – if you have not already done so – installing smoke alarms, putting up a simple carbon monoxide detector and purchasing a domestic fire extinguisher. Obviously, the baby isn't going to crawl down the stairs on her first visit, so focus initially on making sure that the house is generally safe. Remember, too, about the hazard of old lead paint – never attempt to strip paint when the mother-to-be is there, or prior to or during the baby's stay. The accidental consumption of even a few flakes of such paint can cause a child to be severely poisoned.

After the Birth

When the baby is about three months old, start to consider the specific hazards of your home and garden. There are usually a few months to go before the child can crawl, but don't delay your safety measures until it is too late.

Stairs: Babies and young children adore playing on stairs, so be prepared always to supervise them, or else erect stair gates that adults can open and shut but that very effectively contain toddlers. These are quite easy to fit and needn't damage your walls.

Toys: Tidy these after use to avoid you or your grandchildren tripping on them. Consider the safety of any toy you buy, also ensuring that it is for the correct age bracket.

High chairs: Use the lap strap or harness and avoid leaving young children unsupervised in high chairs.

Medicines: Keep all medicines in high, locked cupboards. Cosmetics also should be out of reach.

Baths: Run the cold water before the hot, or – if you have a mixer tap – run the hot and cold together. Close the bathroom door while the bath runs. Use a non-slip mat in the bath and never leave young children unattended in the bath even for a moment.

Lavatories: Get into the habit of always putting the lid down after use.

Household fluids: Bleach, detergents and household cleaners should be kept in cupboards with child-resistant catches, or put up on high shelves out of reach.

Matches, knives and scissors: Keep these out of reach and remember to avoid leaving them around, even for a second.

Cookers: Fit a hob guard to avoid pots falling off, but be sure to remember it is there, otherwise it can knock the bottom of pots and make them spill. Pan handles should always be turned to the back. It can be very difficult to buy oven guards, so ensure that you are around and vigilant when the oven is on. Also, test food before you serve it, to ensure that it is not too hot.

Fridges and freezers: Where the doors are accessible to children, fit these with child-resistant locks.

Electricity: Discourage babies and children from touching electrical equipment, and place plastic plug-in covers over any open power points. Remember that electric heaters are particularly dangerous, and preferably don't use them at all with children around.

Electric kettles: Push flexes to the back of the kitchen surfaces where children can't tug on them. Ideally, purchase coiled flexes (like telephone leads) for greater safety.

Hot drinks: Keep these well out of the reach of children at all times and never put them down on the floor.

Fires: Cover all fires – open and artificial – with childproof fireguards that can be fixed to the wall.

Radiators: As a temporary measure, cover these with towels. For more permanent (and effective) safety, fix a radiator guard (like those in playgroups and schools).

Doors: If these have thin glass panes, consider covering them with safety film – on both sides. Be careful of trapping small fingers in door hinges and always close doors slowly. Guards are now becoming available to prevent fingers from being inserted.

Windows: Avoid opening lower windows, or install safety catches that allow them only to be opened a little way.

Furniture and furnishings: Be aware of any sharp corners or points, which can be particularly hazardous when babies are learning to walk. Small plastic adhesive semi-circles can be bought which cover any corners, and do not harm the furniture (or the child!).

Surfaces and tables: Never put a Moses basket, bouncing cradle or car seat up on to a surface, as the baby's wriggling can make these move (or you might accidentally knock them off).

Beds: Never leave babies and young children unattended on beds as they can easily roll off. If they nap on the bed, put a couple of pillows on either side of them to stop them from rolling, and be sure to be there when they wake up. Also, carefully supervise 'bouncing on the bed' games (which so often end in bouncing *off* the bed).

Plastic bags: Keep these out of reach of children and *never* allow them to be used as play objects.

Pets: Be careful your grandchild doesn't fancy your pets' food or drink. Feed animals outside, if you can, or else where the food is inaccessible to the child. Similarly, keep litter trays out of a toddler's way. Keep potentially aggressive pets well away from children.

Cars: Play music and story tapes, or give children books to avoid their distracting you while you drive. Ensure that car seats are properly secured in the back of the car, and that the children are correctly strapped in.

Safety in the Garden

All children love to play outside, so the first thing your grandchild will do – just as soon as he or she can crawl – is explore your garden, if you have one. Obviously you will accompany the child, but it only takes a moment's inattention for accidents to happen, so the safer the environment can be made, the better.

If you have temporarily to leave a baby sleeping in the garden, ensure that it is covered with an insect net, and safe from cats. Try not to use pesticide, weed killer or fertilizer before children visit, and avoid putting down slug pellets and other edible hazards.

Water features: No matter how small, water features, such as ponds and pools, are an obvious danger. Fence around them, or cover them with a wood and wire frame before there is any question of the child being able to fall into them.

Sheds: Those containing tools, fertilizers, etc. should be kept locked. If the child does want to explore a shed, then an adult must be in attendance all the time.

Gates: As soon as the child arrives at your home, any gate that leads out on to a road or other dangerous area should be kept shut and locked with a childproof lock (e.g. a chain and padlock).

Plants: Be aware of which trees and plants are poisonous – like laburnum, ivy berries, etc. Train your grandchild not to eat anything from the garden, unless you pick and present it! Pull up and safely dispose of all fungi.

Paddling pools: Supervise children at all times, and when they have finished, empty the pool and turn it upside down.

Sandpits: Ensure that the sand is not so deep that a child could become buried in it, and cover the pit when not in use.

Safe Habits

Ask the parents to update you on your grandchild's abilities so as to keep one step ahead. Then look at your house and garden from the child's point of view, and don't just think about what *might* be made safer – as the phrase goes, *DO IT NOW*. You could ask the parents to help with anything you can't manage on your own.

Similarly, it is up to us not to increase the natural hazards of our grandchildren's environment by buying our grandchildren unsuitable gifts. When buying toys for them, try to choose items with a safety standard label, and if you do buy any cheap ones (children are apt to *adore* cheap toys), make sure that no part of the toy is liable to cause harm. It is a common complaint from young parents that they have to remove potentially hazardous toys bought by grandparents, and then bear with the misery this confiscation causes.

It goes without saying that you shouldn't smoke around your grandchildren, as passive smoking can be harmful to them (especially to those with asthma). You must be particularly careful not to take new babies into a smoky environment. Most grandparents say that they will have the odd drink when the parents are there, but not even one when they are in sole charge, and this does seem a sensible precaution.

Right from the start, teach your grandchild road sense. When you come to a road, don't just saunter across it, but demonstrate through your own behaviour the sort of caution they should come to exercise. Morover, where roads are concerned, don't give them the benefit of the doubt. Lock garden gates, hold hands tightly, carry an active toddler. Better to be over-cautious than laissez-faire.

Obviously, we can't move everything out of the children's way, but we can move the move dangerous and precious things. If we don't, then we haven't much right to be angry if accidents happen or our possessions get broken or spoilt. At the same time, the parents should remain vigilant and do their part in keeping an eye on what their offspring are up to.

Don't let all these dos and don'ts daunt you – remember, it all happens very gradually. But try not to get impatient with any advice the parents may give you about child safety. Ultimately, they are in charge of their children's well-being, so however fussy you may think them, always give them the benefit of the doubt.

Some Thoughts and Experiences

'As soon as I knew my daughter-in-law was pregnant, I started worrying about the pool in the garden, which, wouldn't you know, I had not long completed and was very proud of. It was quite big, and I really didn't want to get rid of it entirely, so I consulted my local gardening expert. He suggested I put a low fence with a little gate around it, and that's what I've done. To make this fence attractive I've grown plants over it and it actually looks quite pretty. It means we can take Daniel in to have a look at the fish, but we can shut the gate and relax when he's toddling around the rest of the garden.'

'The house we live in is on the top of a hill and, although it is on a country road, traffic flies past at a terrible pace and there is no pavement. We normally leave the gate open because it makes it much easier for anyone turning into our drive, but, whenever the grandchildren come, or any other children for that matter, we shut the gate and lock it with a child-proof padlocked chain.'

'As her son grew more adventurous, my daughter worried in case he might try to open any of our bedroom windows. They live on the ground floor and therefore all sorts of things about having an upper floor fascinate our grandchildren. I phoned for a man to come and fit locks on the windows. He didn't turn up and the family was due to arrive any minute. So I nailed the windows so that they can only open half an inch. At this very moment we are having a bedroom window replaced because it is made of a single sheet of unstrengthened glass, and a child bouncing on a bed could smash straight through it. All of these things cost money and time, of course, but where young children are concerned it is essential to cross bridges well before you come to them.

'Such issues bring us face to face with the age-old dilemma of protecting children sufficiently, without making them unable to negotiate danger. It's a difficult one and, like many other quandaries concerning children, there is no simple answer. But, so far as we're concerned, it makes sense to us to fix anything in our house that may be a potential hazard. We would never forgive ourselves if anything happened to the grandchildren through our negligence. Making the adjustments has the added bonus of helping us to relax much more when they are here. It's a happier atmosphere for the children, too, if the grown-ups don't have to keep nagging them.'

'I think that to go as far as emptying our garden shed of all gardening tools and hiding them away would be excessively cautious. We hang them high, tell the children not to go near them and explain why. So far that has worked, although we always accompany them if they go into the shed. Children cannot have every single hazard removed from them, and it is only too easy to become obsessive, especially if you have a vivid imagination. But you have to try to keep a balance. Quite ordinary things can potentially be very dangerous, but are easy to render safe, like children's shoelaces (a reason to bless Velcro fasteners). At the moment there is a public service film on television warning people to pick up toys left lying around – an attempt on behalf of the Government to prevent the thousands of household accidents caused by this, not only to children but to grown-ups, too. Now it's become second nature with us to clear away toys and put any coffees or cups of tea up on the mantelpiece rather than on a lower surface, but I have to admit I had to get used to doing it all again. I had forgotten just how quick children can be, and my daughter had to re-train me.'

'Apparently, a large percentage of scalded children who come into casualty departments have been burnt by hot drinks left carelessly within reach.'

'In winter we usually have an open coal fire, but when the children come, we turn up the central heating, the fire remains unlit and the fender is padded with old cushions.'

'I dread taking them to their house. His mother likes knick-knacks and has them all spread about on tiny tables. She has a china collection on the sideboard – the house is just like an antiques shop. With two boys under the age of four, I spend my time there unable to relax in the slightest. My younger one disappeared for a second and returned holding a little Wedgwood bowl in his hands. I said, "Give that to Mummy, there's a good boy" and reached out – but too late. He dropped it on the kitchen tiles. Granny was furious, and although she tried to pretend it was all right, she did it in a huffy sort of way. I'm sorry it happened, but why can't she just move her best things out of the boys' reach on the few occasions we visit? Then we could all relax.'

'Very often, when my daughter and her husband come, they are so tired and spaced out with lack of sleep that they relax too much and leave the care of the children entirely to me, which is difficult if I'm also trying to cook a meal for them. It's not so bad if my husband is there too, but if he is, then the young parents give up completely and just sit reading

> newspapers while we run about like demented hens trying
> to stop the grandchildren from wrecking the joint. I suppose
> you can't blame them, parenting is hard work and I like
> them to relax, but I do get a bit cross sometimes when they
> don't try to stop our grandson from ruining the video
> recorder. We've had to have it mended twice and it cost
> a fortune.'

First Aid

The importance of up-to-date knowledge of first aid cannot be
over-emphasized. Many out-dated practices (like putting butter
on a burn) can actually be harmful, and obviously where their
grandchildren are concerned, all grandparents will want to know
the latest life-saving techniques. This information can be obtained
in courses run by St John's Ambulance Society and elsewhere, as
well as from any one of the several excellent books on the subject
available. Your local library or Yellow Pages are good first ports of
call for helping you obtain information on current practices.

Index